LISBON

A view from the »Castelo de São Jorge« to the »Praça do Comércio« on the Rio Tejo

»Azulejo« decoration in the »Cervejaria da Trindade«

Morning mood on the »Praça Luís de Camões« in the shopping district »Chiado«

Modern entertainment is staged in the old »Coliseu dos Recreios«

L I S B O N

Photos and Text
Manfred Hamm · Werner Radasewsky

Nicolaische Verlagsbuchhandlung Berlin

This book was published with the support of the »Câmara Municipal de Lisboa«

Cover photo: Statue of the »São Vicente«
and View of the »Igreja e Mosteiro de São Vicente« as
well as the cupola of the »Panteão Nacional«
Photo page 10: Group of figures led by Infante Dom
Henrique, part of the »Padrão dos Descobrimentos«
(Discovered Monument)
Back cover photo:
Sign in the »Estoril« station of the City Train line

2nd revised edition, 1989
©1988 Nicolaische Verlagsbuchhandlung
Beuermann GmbH, Berlin
All rights reserved
Translation from the German version, »Lissabon«, 1988:
Mitch Cohen
Layout: Peter Senftleben
Maps: Ingo Naroska
Typesetting: Nagel Fototype, Berlin
Offset Lithography: O.R.T. Kirchner + Graser GmbH,
Berlin
Printing and Dust Jacket: Passavia GmbH, Passau
Printed in Germany

ISBN 3-87584-246-4

Getting to know a city is more than merely knowing its place-names and more than locating its sights, main streets, and business centers, more than experiencing its gastronomy and its pulse. It means concerning oneself with its development through history as well as with the life and doings of its inhabitants and with their moods, until one has a feel for nuances.

To really get to know a city, one must almost conspire with it; not merely following the explications of a guide, one should take a glimpse behind the scenes; this is indispensable.

Many people, visitors and tourists, enjoy their visits to foreign cities while ignoring the manner in which life is lived there and the history behind the city's place-names. Instead, memories of a city are formed by some souvenir or other that the visitor has purchased.

Cities are sometimes cold and distanced, closed and even hostile – just as they can convey security, openness, and much human cooperation. Cities are, indeed, always mirrors of their inhabitants.

Lisbon is a very accessible city. It meets its visitors halfway; they in turn soon feel animated to respond in kind. Lisbon is in no way a rough city; it is open and has at its disposal the substance of a true capital.

At the same time, it has staked out its dimensions with moderation, and thus has been able to retain its cordiality.

Lisbon's flair is slightly intoxicating. The Atlantic light, the temperament of the »Lisboetas«, all the old alleys and nooks, all the sights and monuments; commerce, too, and the bustle and everyday rhythms of the inhabitants, all contribute to the creation of this mood – as does, of course, the traditionally excellent cuisine. Cheerfulness, friendliness, and hospitality round out this impression.

He who becomes acquainted with Lisbon will have unforgettable experiences.

This book reveals some particularities of Lisbon, and does it in its own, very individual way – through someone who has long known Lisbon well, and who has become, through knowledge of the fate of the city, its intimate expert and friend.

Accompany him on the following pages, take pleasure in the excellent photographs, and enjoy this invitation to Lisbon.

Câmara Municipal de Lisboa
O Vereador
Víctor Gonçalves

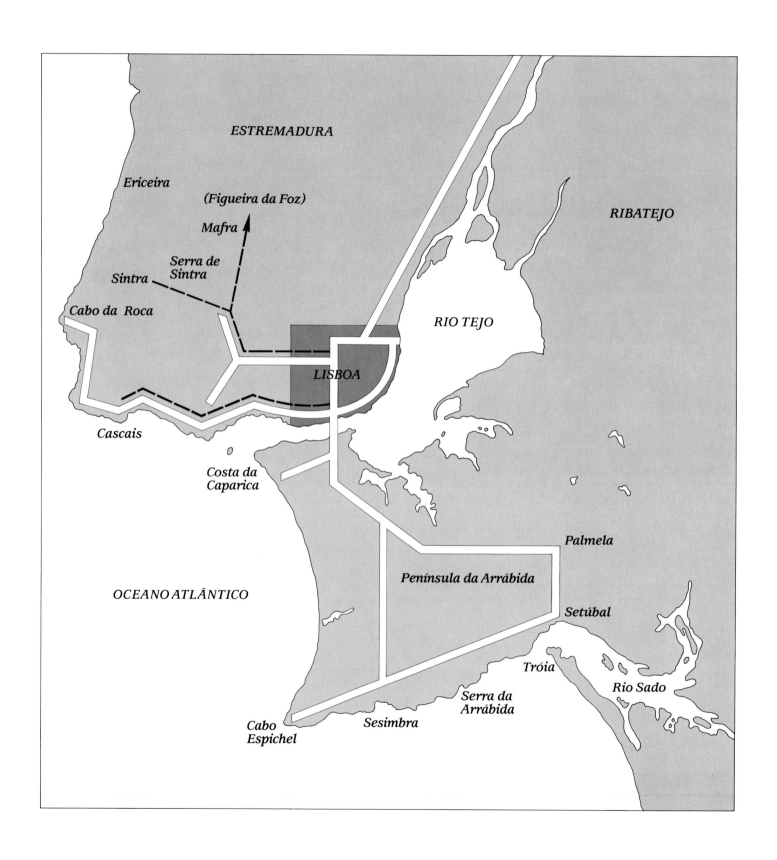

LISBON AND ITS SURROUNDINGS

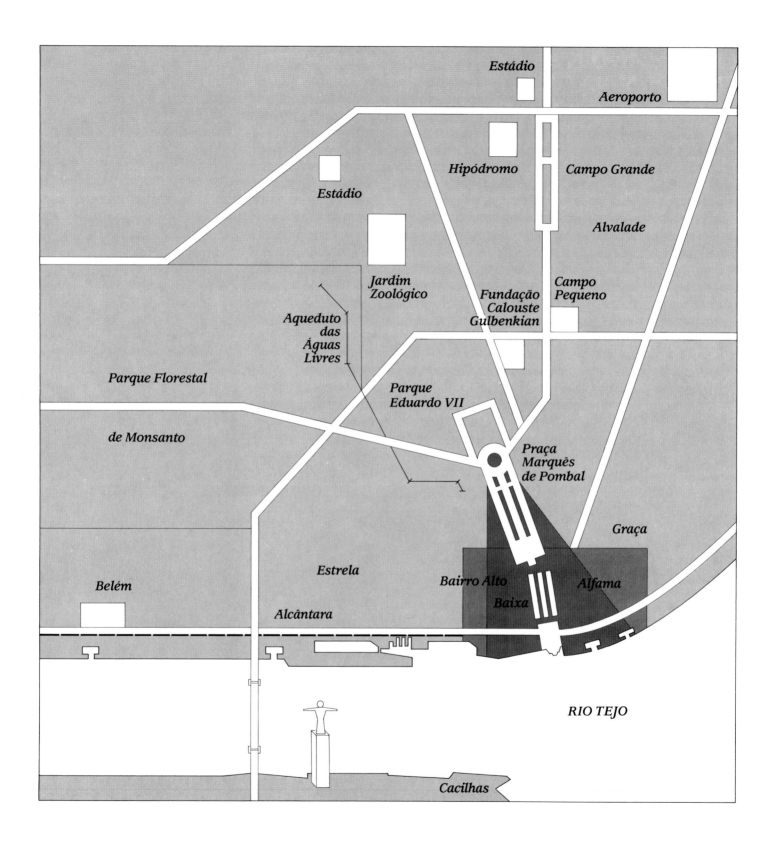

The Center

In the Triangle between the Praça Marquês de Pombal, the Avenida da Liberdade, and the Praça do Comércio; at the Cais do Sodré and through the Baixa across the Bairro Alto – a Historical Excursion back to the Earthquake of 1755.

In the middle of Lisbon, »em Lisboa«! For the Lisboans, the »Lisboetas«, that is the »Rossio« plaza and the »Praça da Figueira«; it is the »Avenida da Liberdade« and the lower city, laid out in right angles – the »Baixa«. The »Praça do Comércio« and the »Praça Marquês de Pombal« are as noticeable landmarks as the shopping district »Chiado« or the Old City »Alfama« with the »Castelo de São Jorge«. Using a map of the city, first-time visitors to this port on the Atlantic are quickly acquainted with these placenames. But it takes much longer to become familiar with the city itself. A map can hardly convey how hilly and even mountainous the intricate Portuguese capital is, in its extent along the Rio Tejo to the broad ocean.

The »Praça dos Restauradores« is a recommended point of departure for exploring, and even Lisbon's old hands start here when they fall once more under the spell of the bustling vitality of this dignified Atlantic metropolis.

An obelisk reaches upward in the middle of the »Praça dos Restauradores«. The monument represents the Portuguese people's desire and will for an independent Portugal. The nation has never forgotten that their affairs were run by Spanish regents from 1580 to 1640. The name of the »Avenida da Liberdade«, which stretches uphill from the »Praça dos Restauradores«, commemorates the thirst for freedom of the inhabitants of Europe's oldest nation-state.

The »Avenida«, as it is known colloquially, empties into the »Praça Marquês de Pombal«. If an acute triangle were laid over the map of the city from this point, it would cover a large part of the downtown area. At the uppermost point of the triangle, more broad streets lead to the »Praça Marquês de Pombal«, whose »Metro« station is called »Rotunda«. One side of the imaginary triangle leads from this magnificent inner city fulcrum along the »Avenida«, Lisbon's most dazzling street, down to the Rio Tejo. Beautiful plazas are touched on and the »Baixa« as well as the »Alfama« come into view. On the imposing »Praça do Comércio« the line bends, paralleling the Rio Tejo up to the bustling »Cais do Sodré«, leading through the elegant »Chiado« shopping district, through the pulsing »Bairro Alto«, back up to the »Praça Marquês de Pombal«.

In the following pages, this imaginary downtown-triangle will be introduced more closely, though not all

too systematically. The differences in elevation, the intricate streets, and above all the life of Lisbon cannot be discovered by prescribed plan. Lisbon invites tours of discovery and holds surprises in store even for its long-time fans.

The »Avenida da Liberdade« is 1.5 kilometers long and about 100 meters wide. Tall trees grow between the main traffic lanes and the supplementary lanes to the right and left. The »Avenida« owes its permanent green to the palms and the flower beds along the wide sidewalks. Here, chic young people stroll, businessmen go for walks during their lunch break, and pedestrians dash daringly to the other side of the street through fast-moving traffic. Tourists admire the beautiful mosaics on the pavement and swans even groom their feathers in the little watercourses. The »Avenida« is lined with splendid houses, sidewalk cafés, and cinemas like the »Tivoli«, with its artistically restored cupola and the typically Lisboan newsstand in front. Hiding across the street is the entrance to the popular »Parque Mayer«. Recently some old buildings with »Avenida visages« are giving way to a newer architecture with glittering facades. Behind them are shopping centers or offices. The »Avenida« is regarded as the prime address for domestic and foreign branches of all lines of business.

The »Avenida« has been able to retain its individuality. It is neither extravagant nor superficially adapted to the appetite of tourists for souvenirs. In a »Ginjinha«, a kind of stand-up bar, the liqueur of the same name is still reasonably priced and is consumed by the »Lisboetas«.

Side streets go off at right angles from both sides of the »Avenida da Liberdade«, sometimes slightly downhill, but mostly steeply uphill. The »Avenida« lies in a valley and has its own ups and downs. All around, a densely-built hill landscape unfolds. Even the most exact map of the city cannot reproduce this topography. Daily life streams in waves down the narrow side streets into the »Avenida«. The cosmetic treatment often applied to her »sisters« in other European metropoles would be unbecoming to this showcase street.

The »Rossio« is »the« Lisbon downtown plaza. At the »Hora de Ponta« – during rush hour – crowds of people, busses, taxis, cars, vegetable carts, and chestnut push-carts entangle, knot, and knit hopelessly among each other. Balloon vendors thread their thin-skinned wares through the confusion, and only the pigeons avoid collision. Like the two wheels of an axle, two cafés face each other on the »Rossio«: the »Suiça« (Switzerland) and the café »Nicola«. The »Suiça« is as turbulent as a train station, and this impression is strengthened by the fact that the café has two front ends. On the other side, one finds oneself on the beautiful »Praça da Figueira«, a plaza directly bordering on the »Rossio«. The semicircular script »Nicola« above the entrance invites one into one of the former literary cafés. It is easy to imagine that Fernando Pessoa may once have sat here too, sunk deep in work on the Kafkaesque gloom of his novel *The Book of the Restlessness of the Assistant Bookkeeper Bernardo Soares.*

Behind an archway in the Rua dos Sapateiros, which starts directly from the »Rossio«, an old cinema is hidden. Films have been shown in the »Animatógrafo do Rossio« since 1907. Since that time, virgins bear shining electric lamps on both sides of the richly ornamented entrances, a truly glowing greeting to the new electric epoch, here also immortalized on »Azulejos« (tiles).

The calm eye of the storm of the »Rossio«, whose core is held auto-free, is comprised of the colorful flower stands and the two fountains. In the middle of the plaza, a monument stretches upward from the pedestrian zone, artistically paved in wavy lines. On the marble column is the likeness of Dom Pedro IV. The »Rossio« is officially named »Praça Dom Pedro IV« after this Portuguese king, who was also Emperor of Brazil for a time.

The tour of the city can continue upward to the »Praça Marquês de Pombal« or downward through the »Baixa« to the Rio Tejo. In both cases, the name »Pombal« recalls Lisbon's new beginning after the natural catastrophe of November 1, 1775. It was All Souls' and many people were in the churches when a terrible earthquake split the earth for 10 minutes at 9 in the morning. Afterwards, nothing was the same as before. The city had been razed. In Europe's richest city, thousands of plazas, churches, cloisters, and houses were destroyed. About 60,000 deaths were mourned. In our time, the strength of the earthquake of 1775 was investigated. Geophysicists estimate its violence at between 8.5 and 9 on the Richter scale.

The man of the hour was the later Marquês de Pombal. King José I gave free rein to his Secretary of State, who was afterward raised to the nobility as Marquês. With his legendary motto, »Sepultar os mortos, cuidar dos vivos, fechar os portos« – »Bury the dead, care for the living, close the ports« – the Rationalist and Enlightenment man Pombal went to work. For the first time in modern Europe, a city was systematically envisioned on the drawing boards of architects: square-cornered, checkerboard in form – the future »Manhattan« pattern. The »Cidade Pombalina« was and is a triumph of city planning and construction. The broad streets were paved. A sewage system was laid out. The four- and five-storey buildings have cellars. The Marquês de Pombal set up a building code for further housing, just as he instigated other intelligent legislation and promoted government initiative for the welfare of the population – to the benefit of all of Portugal, and, in many fields, for the first time anywhere in Europe. The »Baixa«, as this downtown Lisbon area is called today, is simultaneously functional, stately, and timeless. The central Rua Augusta has been converted to a pedestrian mall where pavement painters, peddlers, street artists, cafés, and stores cater to visitors from far and wide.

The »Arco Monumental« connects the »Baixa« with the magnificent »Praça do Comércio«, undoubtedly one of the best-designed plazas in Europe. On the open side, a stairway descends to the Rio Tejo. The three remaining borders of the square »Comércio« are clean-lined, densely-built, and lined with arcades. In the Northeastern corner, the »Café Restaurante Martinho da Arcada« is almost hidden, a haunt of the writer Fernando Pessoa. A monument to King Dom José I was erected in the middle of the plaza; high on his horse, he gazes at the stretch of the Rio Tejo where, during the earthquake of 1775, it overflowed its banks and flooded large parts of the city.

Dom José I is called the »Reformador«. Under his aegis, the Marquês de Pombal began the rebuilding of Lisbon and a modern transformation of the Portuguese state. The harmonious unity of the »Praça do Comércio«, the former center of commerce between river and city, had already existed in another form before 1775. Until then, the royal residence had been on the plaza, which is still known popularly as the »Terreiro do Paço« (palace terraces).

The Rio Tejo has always played a role. It begins in Spain as the Rio Tajo, but is really a »Portuguese river«.

Model of Lisbon before the Earthquake of 1755.
The »Terreiro do Paço« was rebuilt on the Rio Tejo
as the »Praça do Comércio«

It is navigable only in Portugal, and the history of Lisbon and, indeed, all of Portugal, is closely bound up with it. From Lisbon, such Portuguese seafarers as Vasco da Gama, Pedro Álvares Cabral, Diogo Cão, or Bartolomeu Dias left Europe's largest river mouth for the ocean, conquering other continents and new worlds for trade and for Christendom. They sailed back to the city on the Rio Tejo and contributed to its 16th century emergence as Europe's most thriving metropolis. –

Pedestrians stream endlessly to the »Terminal Fluvial«. Those are the boat stations »Terreiro do Paço« and »Cais da Alfândega«, slightly offset from the »Comércio«, which service the orange/white and blue ferries. They steer to the other side of the Tejo and to Barreiro, where one of Lisbon's four main train stations is reached after a 40-minute crossing. The »Cacilheiros« dock near the »Comércio«, as well, before cruising to Cacilhas and the great state shipyard »Lisnave«. Many excellent fish restaurants beckon in Cacilhas.

Not far from the »Praça do Comércio«, City Hall stands on the intimate »Praça do Município«. This impressive building, from which the mayor, the »Presidente da Câmara Municipal de Lisboa«, administers the city, is a neoclassical structure from the second half of the 19th century. »Os Paços do Concelho« fully unfold their architectonic charm in the building's interior.

In the middle of the City Hall square, three braided columns twist upward from a pedestal. This is a »Pelou-

20

rinho« and was erected to symbolize that a community had the rights of a free city. In Lisbon, this was the case from 1392 on.

The shore road »Ribeira das Naus« bends westward at the »Praça do Comércio« and leads to the lively »Cais do Sodré«. Here is another ferry station, from where, on board the »Cacilheiros«, one is offered breathtaking views of Lisbon; the city railroad (»Linha«) to genteel Estoril and Cascais has its end points at the »Cais do Sodré«, and here are the central marketplaces. In their central location reminiscent of the legendary and longsince demolished »Les Halles« of Paris, these are perhaps unique in Europe today. Up through the 1930's the same purpose was served by the completely roofed-over »Praça da Figueira«, neighboring the »Rossio«.

Between 2 and 3 in the morning, life begins in the »belly of Lisbon«. From Estremadura, the province extending from Lisbon to the North, small trucks roll incessantly to provide the metropolis and the Lisboetas with all their groceries. With salad, »Alface«, as well, of course. The Lisboetas have a special relationship to this leafy vegetable. The Lisboans call themselves »Alfacinhas«, which means as much as »little head of lettuce«. And a true Lisboan, one who was born in Lisbon, is called an »Alfacinha de Gema« – »a little head of lettuce with yolk«. Fruit, meat, vegetables, and of course freshly caught fish and shellfish (»Mariscos«) are displayed in the market halls and in the shacks directly on the pier. The »Vareiras« balance their freight of sardines on their heads in their broad, plate-shaped »Canastra«, a basket like a wagon wheel. The »black women« – clothes, hair, and skin color are black – belong to the »Cais do Sodré« and its »Mercado da Ribeira«, as do the strolling newspaper vendors on the stairs of the railroad building.

Following the imaginary triangle laid over the center, one turns from the »Cais do Sodré«, leaving the Rio Tejo behind, and follows the steeply climbing Rua do Alecrim past the gate-like viaducts upward to the shopping district »Chiado« and into the »Bairro Alto«, the »Upper City«; topographically, this district is the antithesis of the »Baixa«, the »Lower City«. This most mountainous port city in Europe constantly demands to be climbed.

Halfway up, the road leads past the »Praça Luís de Camões«. This plaza, named after what must be Portugal's greatest author, is simultaneously lost in dreams and surrounded by raging traffic. Over 400 years ago, Luís de Camões wrote Os Lusíadas – The Lusiads, an epic that strikingly depicts Portugal's, and thus the West's, departure into distant and as yet unknown regions.

As the plaza's namegiver, the poet stands, in stone, appropriately in the middle of the »Praça Luís de Camões«, like a Godfather of all bibliophile friends. Nearby bookstores and antique stores beckon with new and old books, woodcuts, engravings, and aquatints.

Steep labyrinthine alleys tempt one to a side-trip down to the »Estação do Rossio«. This train station is an exotic exception among European stations. Huge horseshoe-shaped gateways and window casements trigger associations with Moorish architecture. The »Rossio« station – the former »Estação Central« – is terraced into the mountain, accessible to vehicles only through a long tunnel through the rock. Across the station, which can be reached by foot from all sides, one arrives down in the »Baixa« again. Not far away, the world's most beautiful and original elevator tower stretches into the heights. The filigreed metal bar construction seems to eliminate its weight.

The »Elevador de Santa Justa« is a unique part of the city transport system. Built in 1901 as part of the wave of architectural enthusiasm for the Eiffel Tower, the iron monument's two luxurious wooden cabins take passengers more than 30 meters upward. Raoul Mesnier de Ponsard, a Portuguese of French descent, was responsible for this »Elevador de Santa Justa«. It is less well known that he also built another similar elevator, the »Elevador da Biblioteca«. The »Elevador de Biblioteca« was torn down in 1915. Ponsard was also the constructor of the unusual mountain railways in Nazaré and near Braga (Bom Jesus do Monte).

From the gallery of the »Santa Justa« elevator tower, the terraced »Rossio« station can be recognized; the green of the trees on the »Avenida da Liberdade« glows through the roofs; the »Praça Marquês de Pombal« can be seen; and from here the strict harmony of the »Baixa Pombalina« can be grasped.

Facing the tower from beyond the valley, the »Castelo de São Jorge« stands majestically on the mountain. It crowns the »Alfama«, Lisbon's true Old City. Its buildings survived the terrible earthquake of 1775 almost unscathed.

A footbridge connects the »Elevador de Santa Justa« with the outer part of the »Bairro Alto«, the upper city. The view from the bridge onto the pedestrian street, Rua do Carmo, shows what has changed since August, 1988, when a fire destroyed many Pombaline buildings with their noble shops and historic counting houses. But the »Chiado«, this exclusive shopping area, has kept its face. It adopted the pseudonym of the poet António Ribeiro, who smiles down slyly from his monument. Across the way, his »colleague« Fernando Pessoa has taken a seat as a life-size sculpture on the terrace of the old café »A Brasileira«.

The »Chiado« is also the proud cultural center of Lisbon. Opera and ballet are performed in the »Teatro São Luiz«. The classics are shown in the monumental »Teatro Nacional de São Carlos«. Across from it is the house where Fernando Pessoa was born, Portugal's most important writer in this century (June 13, 1888 – November 30, 1935). The bookstore »Bertrand« in the Rua Garrett is over 300 years old and acts as a magnet for all booklovers.

Not far off, one passes the »Largo do Carmo«. These remnants of a roofless Carmelite church and the remaining Gothic arches are, today, the most noticeable reminders of the earthquake. The »Igreja do Carmo« has been converted into an archaeological museum.

On the way to the Rua da Misericórdia, a visit to the »Cervejaria da Trindade« is recommended. The unique atmosphere consists not only in the size of the great halls of the busy restaurant, but also in the »Trindade's«, many unusual »Azulejo« pictures.

Across the Rua da Misericórdia, one can drift through the rising and falling alleyways of the »Bairro Alto«, where »typical« Lisbon reveals itself.

But what is typical for this city? Lisbon falls into so many urban parts, has so many breaks and contradictions, connects – sometimes smoothly, sometimes awkwardly – its problematical quarters and its beautiful residential areas as does hardly any other large European city. There is no common denominator for all of Lisbon, and the proof is to be seen in every district – including the »Bairro Alto«.

This small quarter has something labyrinthine and confusing, despite its clear street pattern. A »Fado« bar and a public bath and shower facility alternate without ostentation. A bookbinding business, a tavern where wine is tapped from huge barrels, a little fish market, many »Tascas« and »Restaurantes« are examples of the bustling business of the »Bairro Alto« and its inhabitants. Josephine Baker had her favorite bar here, where she also performed, long before she made headlines elsewhere: everything in that »Boîte« is just like it was …

When darkness spreads over Lisbon, life changes in the »Bairro Alto«. During the day, people work in the countless small businesses in order to live. At night, they live and forget work. Then the Beautiful People of »Lisboa« meet in a disco – all in the »dernier cri«. Tourists, too, are let out here for a »Lisbon-by-night« tour; and only the children who play in the streets long into the night or some ladies pursuing their business give an idea of how diverse life is in this area, and of how light and shadow are distributed equally through the »Bairro Alto«. –

On the way to »Praça Marquês de Pombal« and the point of the triangle invisibly drawn over the center, one side-trip takes only a few minutes – or hours! The »Port Wine Institute«, »O Solar do Vinho do Porto«, is right on the edge of the »Bairro Alto«, across from the Calçada da Glória at the upper station of the wedge-shaped, streetcar-like »Elevador da Glória«, which is over 100 years old. (Yet another two such »Elevadores« belong to Lisbon's public transport system – in times past, there were eight mountain and valley railways.)

In 1747, the foundations were laid for what is now the »Solar do Vinho do Porto«, which doesn't seem at all like an »institute«. It is a kind of public wine tavern, even if the overall impression from outside doesn't reveal it. Here one's »Cálice« is filled with great port wines of all vintages, all brands, and all flavors and »Cores« (color nuances). The former »Palácio«, whose doors are now open to port wine afficionados, was built by a German contractor. Later he became a naturalized Portuguese and no longer called himself Johann Friedrich Ludwig, but rather João Frederico Ludovice, the name under which he is known in Portuguese architectural history. He was the builder of the huge Convent in Mafra near Lisbon – constructed at the time in rivalry with the gigantic Spanish »Escorial« near Madrid.

The dreamlike idyll of the »Praça do Príncipe Real« unfolds itself if one follows the Rua de Dom Pedro V with its antique stores. Behind the typical Lisboan newspaper stand with its metal hat, the spreading limbs of a tree are propped up by wrought iron supports. Europe's largest tree crown measures over 25 meters in diameter. From

The structure of the »Baixa« is recognizable from a bird's-eye-view. The »Elevador de Santa Justa« leads to the »Bairro Alto«. In the immediate neighborhood, around the Rua do Carmo and Rua Garett, a part of the noble shopping district, the »Chiado«, was laid to waste by a terrible fire

its shadow, one can watch the crowd at the nearby pond; when it rains, the »Cypressus lusitanica« makes a grandiose umbrella.

The Calçada da Patriarcal winds downward in serpentines beside the »Casa de Macau« – past the Lisbon University's Chancellor's Office with its exotic towers, crenels, and half-arches, past the Rua da Alegria as well. At its end, one finds the small, secretive entrance to the botanical gardens, a horticultural jewel. The much more well known »Jardim Botânico« is called »Estufa Fria« (»Cold Step«) and always amazes its visitors with its immense, seemingly invisible greenhouses. The »Estufa Fria« is located in the Northwestern area of the elongated »Parque Eduardo VII«.

A slight detour leads over the remodeled »Largo do Rato« and from there through the »Arco Grande das Amoreiras«. The streetcars, the »Eléctricos«, run in alternating directions along a single pair of rails through these out-of-the-way triumphal arches, then passing through a giant area of new apartment complexes. At the upper end of the Rua das Amoreiras, Lisbon's most modern shopping center has grown: »Amoreiras«.

The turbulent combination of glass, steel, concrete, and color, distributed among flat buildings, multi-stories, and freeways, not only gave the metropolis an extensive shopping center and office district, but also a new, unmistakable skyline. Tomás Taveira was entrusted with this mammoth project. In modern Lusitanian buildings elsewhere, too, one finds this internationally known architect's postmodernism.

In the Rua Alexandre Herculano, immediately neighboring the »Largo do Rato«, a building monument of quite another kind can be discovered. Since 1906, an auto repair shop has been there with its broad arched roof reminiscent of sacred architecture. Giant »Azulejo« letters refer to this »Auto Palace«, whose further attraction lies in the wonderful stained glass windows with motifs from the beginnings of the automobile era.

One arrives at the »Avenida da Liberdade«. Where it runs into the »Praça Marquês de Pombal«, the sober lines of the building housing the newspaper »O Diário de Notícias« (»D. N.«) can be made out. It is one of the – rather unnoticed – Lisboan buildings reminiscent of the »Bauhaus« tradition. This was the humane direction in architecture and the arts that emerged in Germany in the 1920's and which triggered a rethinking of architectural-esthetic problems. The monument to the Marquês de Pombal in the middle of the »Praça« named for him looks out toward the »Baixa«. The renewer of the city would surely have liked the »D. N.« building, which stands in the immediate vicinity of the columns of the monument. After all, the name Pombal is associated with rethinking and with the project of creating a new and better time. –

At the »Praça Marquês de Pombal«, one has returned to the point of the imaginary triangle originally laid out over the city. The glimpses that Lisbon and its inhabitants have already afforded lead one to suspect that the city holds many more surprises in store.

Gallery and terrace of the »Elevador de Santa Justa«

A view through the pointed arches of the earthquake-damaged »Convento do Carmo« toward the »Praça do Comércio«

25

Creative pause in the Rua Morais Soares

Melon vendor in the market hall at the »Cais do Sodré«

»Praça da Figueira« *with the monument to the founder of the* *»Aviz«* *dynasty, Dom João I*

Statue of the »Marquês de Pombal« in front of the »Parque Eduardo VII«

In the noble shopping district »Chiado«, dignified, elegant shops continue to convey the charm of times past

The »Animatógrafo do Rossio« is one of the oldest European cinemas still in operation

A ›bandleader‹ at the busy »Largo Martim Moniz«

The scissors grinder announces himself with melodious whistles

As if the author Fernando Pessoa was on his way to his regular café on the »Praça do Comércio«. The slender man with the hat and glasses shyly tried to keep his writing a secret. His worldwide fame was posthumous. »Wise is he who keeps his existence monotonous, for then every little incident possesses the privilege of a wonder.« Fernando Pessoa is portrayed for posterity at work in the »Café Restaurante Martinho da Arcada« in the picture by the well-known Portuguese artist, Almada Negreiros

A touch of Moorish architecture on the centrally located train station »Estação do Rossio«

The Portuguese passion for freedom manifests itself on the »Praça dos Restauradores«

Frontal view of the »Igreja e Mosteiro de São Vicente«

A view through the »Arco Monumental« into the pedestrian zone Rua Augusta

The Rio Tejo streams past the »Praça do Comércio« and in front of the monument to King José I

Dignified halls blend into each other in the city hall »Paços do Conselho«

The monument of Dom Pedro IV recalls the official title of the »Rossio«

A new skyline emerges in old Lisbon

43

The royal box in the »Teatro Dona Maria II« is reserved today for the President. This building was erected after the Earthquake of 1755, at the spot on the »Rossio« where the Palace of the Inquisition stood before

In the Middle Ages

The Alfama and the Castelo de São Jorge and Following the Traces of the Romans

The »Alfama« lives in front of and behind the facades, on the stairways, in the narrow, steep, and often winding alleys. From the beginning. For the »Alfama« survived even the earthquake of 1755 nearly unscathed. And so life pulses almost medievally in the roads, often inaccessible to cars, all around the castle peak with its »Castelo de São Jorge«.

Sounds, rhythm, music, scents – especially the smell of sardines grilled on the little »Fogareiros« in front of people's front doors – these determine the impression. Above, on the »Largo de Santa Luzia« and its unique »Miradouro« (viewing terrace), the Old City looks like a conglomeration of rust-brown roofs huddling together, visually clearly separate from the seemingly nearby »Mar de Palha«, the Tejo »straw sea«. The huge Tejo basin has this name because, when the sunlight falls in a certain way, the broad, glittering surface of the water looks like straw that has been set out into the sun to dry.

In Lisbon's true Old City, one goes constantly up and down stone steps; after only a few minutes, one's orientation is lost. Every June 13th in the »Alfama«, joie de vivre overflows through the whole night. A sea of light from innumerable lanterns pours through the intricate net of alleys. Budgies and canaries compete with melodious folk music, and sometimes with a melancholy »Fado« song. The feast of Santo António is being celebrated. He was born in the »Alfama« in 1195 and died, 36 years old, in Padua in Italy, after having performed all sorts of wonders, and was later canonized. He is Lisbon's patron saint. His heart belongs to children, to lovers, and to all who have lost something. –

One dallies in the street of the stockfish anglers, in the Rua dos Bacalhoeiros, in front of the »Casa dos Bicos«. The two missing storeys have been set onto it again. Spiny stones ground like diamonds seem to defend the Renaissance construction (1523) against the rest of the world with hedgehog quills; inside, the presentation of the history of the Portuguese discoverers and discoveries is planned in a new style. These were also depicted by Brás de Albuquerque in his book about his father, *Comentários do Grande Afonso de Albuquerque.* The latter had taken the Asian parts of the known world for Portugal – Goa in India, Malacca in Malaya; he also reached the Moluccan Islands, controlled the trade center Ormuz on the Persian Gulf, and dreamed of a Portuguese colonial empire. The dream became the personal trauma of this self-styled Viceroy of India, for his king Dom Manuel I didn't cooperate with him. With the *Comentários,* his son set him a literary monument and left behind an impressive historical document.

In the turbulent confusion of the »Alfama« it is easy to oversee the survival of »Pátios« – beautiful inner courtyards, often invisible from outside. The »Pátio do Carrasco« from the 15th century mirrors over 300 years of constant remodelling and, thus, of the history of architecture. It bears witness to life before the earthquake, including the inadequate living conditions of the time, and yet radiates a dignity foreign to most modern buildings.

At the »Chafariz d'El Rei«, the peculiar facade-fountain integrated into the wall around the Old City also recalls the long history of the »Alfama« and the inexhaustible vitality of its inhabitants. The Moors initiated the »Al-Hamma« like an eternal flea market; it lives on as the »Alfama«, timeless fountain of youth.

The peak of the »Alfama« is an unmistakable landmark. There, in a semi-circle, the »Castelo de São Jorge« spreads out its outer rings, battlement walls, and stairways. The cheerful atmosphere, the wide view, the calming stillness attract the »Lisboetas« as well as the tourists. Here there is room for all, including for the strange birds in the pheasant aviary. They no longer need fear the dragon slain, legend has it, long, long ago by Saint George, the castle's namegiver (»São Jorge«). Saint George has gone down in church history as the patron of farmers, warriors, and swordsmiths.

Nowadays, the castle's old cannon are only decoration, and the fort has nothing martial about it. Nonetheless, it marks a milestone in Portugal's conflict-ridden history. It is even possible that the Romans layered the first stones for its battlements. During the great European mass migrations, the »Völkerwanderungen«, the Visigoths gained footing here and expanded the strategically-located fortress. But the Moors came, establishing their rule for five centuries. Until 1247. Then they were forced to retreat during the reconquest of Portuguese territory by the »Liberator King« Afonso Henriques. He captured the castle and, from it, proclaimed Lisbon the capital of Europe's first nation-state. Since then Portugal's territorial borders have remained unchanged. Much time passed, constructors and reconstructors have tried their abilities on the »Castelo«, inside and out. The »Terramoto« (earthquake) of 1775 was merciful to the old city »Alfama« and its »Castelo de São Jorge«. The careful renewal of the city on the part of the »Câmara Municipal de Lisboa« will preserve this authentic portion of Luso-European history.

A metropolis had fallen – like Pompeii or Atlantis. The earth had destroyed royal Lisbon and changed the course of the Rio Tejo. But at the same time, nearly 2000 years of Lisboan past were brought almost to the light of day. An old »Lower City« – not the visible, present Lower City, the »Baixa« – was snatched from darkness.

This unknown, underground Lisbon lies even below the »Baixa«. The earthquake had thrust a built-up plateau upward to within a few meters of the present Pombaline street level. It is a labyrinth of rooms, passageways, bridges, main and side hallways, and galleries. Everything is solidly built and well preserved, even though this lower city is almost always under water.

It is an ancient Roman complex and stretches underneath the »Baixa« for hundreds of meters in all directions. The Romans used these constructions as bathhouses, among other things. They have survived the ages almost intact. Huge reservoirs for drinking water testify to impressive logistics and ingenious technical understanding. The total extent of the »Termas Romanas« is unknown.

The baths were discovered during canalization work for the »Baixa«, in the time of the Marquês de Pombal, but were forgotten almost until the present. –

In the Rua da Saudade, the relics of the Roman period in Lisbon are stored in a »Pátio«. The marble columns, capitals, sculptures, blocks, and fragments were found in over twenty points in the city while digging to construct new buildings or the tunnels for the »Metro«. Gradually, a picture is emerging of a Roman city of the 2nd century B.C. A port existed where the downtown area is today, and the palaces, temples, and market buildings were located far to the North of the present inner city.

The Rio Tejo had another course and the coastline was gracefully curved. There must have been a reason why, over three millenia ago, the Phoenicians called the entire coast formation »Gentle Bay« (Ulis Ubbo«). Much later

In the Roman »Termas« below the »Baixa«.
A »Bombeiro Voluntário« leads through the widely-branching arched corridors and connecting canals.
The »Termas Romanas« survived the Earthquake of 1755 almost unscathed

called »Olisippo« or »Olissipum« by the Romans, in Caesar's time the city was called »Felicitas Iulia«, a shorter form of »Urbs municipium civium Romanorum Felicitas Iulia cognominatum«, more or less »Roman Capital of Happy Julia«.

*The old cathedral »Sé« stands on
historical ground. The Moors had already prayed
in a mosque on this spot*

here and, in the following centuries, turned »Al Oshbuna« and »Lishbuna« – today's »Lisboa« – into a thriving trade metropole. –

At the corner of Rua de São Mamede and Rua da Saudade, demolition work preparing for new building exposed the remains of what was probably the most important theater on the Iberian peninsula. As is the case with almost all other Roman relics, the »Teatro Romano« was first exposed by the earthquake. But the post-Pombaline rebuilding used the jumbled theater columns for the construction of new buildings.

Little by little, the »Teatro Romano« has been uncovered. The repertoire in the Roman theater of »Felicitas Iulia« was probably classical theater: no lions, no gladiators. The Romans in their second most important city (after Mérida) in Lusitania, as it was then called, apparently cultivated Lusitanian cheer. The Lusitanians were an ethnic group in the region that is now Northern Portugal. The mixture of original and Latin cultural elements led to the emergence of an autonomous national and cultural identity.

The way back to the present leads, not far from these remnants of Roman history, past a further testimony of the past. The »Sé« is a cathedral, and has the same importance for Lisbon that Notre Dame has for Paris or that the Dome has for Cologne.

»Sé« is the abbreviation of »sedes episcopales«; the »Sé Patriarcal de Lisboa« is also the seat of the bishopric. Today this 13th century structure displays primarily Romanesque features. In the course of the centuries, its appearance has changed to Gothic and to Baroque. Before the founder of the Portuguese state, king Dom Afonso Henriques, had a Christian fortress-church built, the Moors had prayed facing Mecca in a mosque on this same spot. (In the years following 1985, a new and architecturally magnificent mosque has been built. It is elevated above the »Praça de Espanha« and is the first Lisboan mosque in about 700 years.) –

In other places, the great Catholic houses of worship represent spectacular architectonic events. The »Sé« is comparatively modest. Instead of high, pointed towers, here massive flying buttresses are crowned with crenels. Inside, the church is almost empty; during a walk through the quiet cloisters in the inner courtyard, calmness and shadow complement each other in a meditative refreshment from the turmoil outside the gates of the »Sé«.

After the Romans were driven out by other invaders around 410 A.D., the Alans, the Germanic Suebians, and, in 585, the Visigoths came. These called the port city »Ulixiponna« until 713, when the Arabs (Moors) settled

Underway in the Eléctrico

Tours of the City

Somewhat East of the actual downtown area, the road goes past the »Sé« toward »Graça«. This district is situated on the heights and can be reached with the streetcar, the »Eléctrico«. In times past, the whole city was criss-crossed by innumerable lines. About a dozen have survived. The city government (»Câmara Municipal de Lisboa«) had second thoughts before completely eliminating the »Eléctrico«, as was done in so many other large European cities.

The entire transportation and communication network was formerly in British hands. That's why one still sees occasional old English double-decker »Leyland« buses on the streets, why one still finds some typically English telephone booths, and that is why the driver's cabin in the »Eléctrico« has so many little metal signs and cast iron plaques reading »Made in England«. The exterior of the »Eléctrico« is beautifully old-fashioned.

Small, agile, squeaky, wood-panelled, and comfy, Line 28, winds out from »Prazeres« down into the »Baixa« and from there to new heights toward »Graça« (almost like the cable cars in San Francisco). In Lisbon, the »Eléctrico« is truly a streetcar! It hauls along a narrow-gauge track with tight curve radii through the dilapidated pavement. The driver works like a captain at the two silver wheels – and with the same feeling of responsibility! The »Eléctrico« mustn't fall from the steep streets, nor in the tight curves; it must be maneuvered past the vendors' stands, and mustn't scratch the walls of buildings; it must let dogs, cats, and children pass. The driver must take care when passing colleagues where sets of track are close together. At particularly difficult points, men hired to regulate the »Eléctrico« traffic stand with what look like ping-pong paddles. One side is green, for »Go!«, the other side carries the symbol for »No Entrance«. Traffic is regulated by the principle of »First come, first served« – and according to the mood of the man with the paddle. He slips into the entrance of a »Tasca« and keeps eye contact with one colleague downhill to the left, and with another uphill to the right. The strategic points in the narrow, serpentine streets are manned spiritedly by these paddle men. At night, the paddle is replaced by a small oil torch in a heavy metal lantern. Red and green glass filters the torch's light to signal in the appropriate directions. The handsome lantern hangs from the wall of a building on a simple wire; the lanterns are custom-made and about 100 years old –

as old as Lisbon's streetcar system. It is said that no lantern has ever run out of oil and that no standing or sitting paddle man station was ever left unoccupied.

At the corner Escardinhas das Escolas Gerais on the extended Rua Voz do Operário, Line 28 passes a paddle man. Shortly thereafter, elbows must be withdrawn from the »Eléctrico's« open windows; the walls of the surrounding buildings are within arm's reach. The privacy of the ground floor apartments is disturbed with each passing »Eléctrico« – thoroughly and lastingly, for Lisbon's public transportation system is characterized by frequent runs well into the night. The »Eléctrico« always runs with a 2-man crew: the driver, who stands or leans against a crossbar, and the conductor, constantly moving up and down the car. The unwritten rule is: entrance in the back, exit in front. Passengers pull on a bell wire when they want to get out.

Many strangers have great difficulties when they want to ride the streetcar. The »normal« stops on the street curbs are for buses only. Where »Eléctricos« stop, a little white sign with black letters reading »Paragem« (halting point) hangs on a wire in the middle of the street, above the tracks. If the sign swings between the two sets of tracks, the station is for both directions. Underway, the tracks are switched by hand except at extremely busy nodes of streetcar traffic, where switchmen sit in tiny booths at the curb. Every once in awhile, the rod tapping electricity springs off of the cable. And almost every trip intermittently goes in reverse, for the »Eléctrico« is a vehicle like any other; »Eléctrico« drivers have enough insight to see that, in narrow streets, insisting upon the right-of-way is no way to relieve a traffic jam. Sometimes the passengers have to lend a hand moving a car parked too close to the tracks.

Line 28 rides toward »Graça«, snaking its way up the hill. At the beginning of the Rua Voz do Operário, a mighty building commands attention. »Voz do Operário« stands twice in large letters on the front of the building – »Voice of the Worker«. By now, this voice has been replaced by many little voices. The »Voz do Operário« now houses kindergartens. The monumental building, framed by two columns and boasting a glass rosette under the roof, represents the Lisbon mixture of Neoclassicism, Art Nouveau, and the esthetics of wrought iron, especially in the interior. In the hall-like foyer above, this forgotten Portuguese construction style is wedded to a

*Up and down the hills between »Cais do Sodré«
and the »Chiado«*

happy children's world in a grandiose ensemble of old architecture and new life.

The steep Rua Voz do Operário flattens out at the peak of the hill. Sometimes the »Eléctrico« 28 runs further to »Martim Moniz«, sometimes it ends here at the triangularly twined and somehow cock-eyed »Largo da Graça«. The heavy traffic is like everywhere else, yet somehow the businesses and storefronts reveal that this is a workers' district. That wasn't always the case.

The »good« citizens, tradesmen, and craftsmen lived in the shadow of the immense and historically important church and abbey »São Vicente de Fora« and the city royal palaces, situated somewhat lower. Around the turn of the century, »Graça« became proletarian. »Graça« still evidences unique and rather hidden workers' colonies. One built as a »Pátio«, one as a street, one as a remodelled palace. Near the Rua dos Sapadores, the »Vila Rodrigues«, a »Pátio« with two- and three-storey buildings, opens onto Rua Senhora da Glória 142. The structures are connected with a complicated weaving of stairways and galleries. It seems less confusing here than in a similar settlement not far away in the Rua Senhora do Monte, where in 1908 an industrialist built a three-storey complex for »his« workers, equipped all around with wrought iron verandas and balconies. Not far from the »Vila Rodrigues« (»vila« can mean »villa« as well as »city« or »town«) one reaches the »Vila Bertha«. The road to this most pleasant of all Lisbon's workers' colonies leads through the Rua do Sol à Graça to the Travessa da Pereira. The complex was erected in 1902, but has nothing of the miserable »rented barracks« quality of this period's buildings in so many other large European cities.

A side-trip by foot leads north around the »Alfama«. If one keeps to the descending roads, one will almost necessarily land somewhere in the »Baixa«. Across from the »Igreja Convento da Graça«, a »caracol« descends in a spiral from »Graça«, leading past 16th century buildings of great importance at that time: the pottery works (»Lagares«) and olive oil refineries (»Olarias«). »Lagares« and »Olarias« are still there (at least as street names), but not the »Mouraria«. That was the Moorish-Arabic Old City, comparable to the »Alfama«. The »Caracol da Graça« runs in the area of the former Muslim city, which has meanwhile been remodelled and rebuilt. This quarter, not at all in conformity with the rest of the city's building style, is called »Martim Moniz«, after a knight of an order. He and his followers revolted against the Moors and took this terrain for the Christian clergy. The Muslims had buried their dead approximately at the foot of the »Caracol da Graça«. The »Largo do Martim Moniz« and its surroundings are still colloquially called the »Mouraria«. Here one again crosses the »Eléctrico« Line 28. –

A ride on Line 25/26 is perfect for getting to know the usually 24- or 40-seat streetcars without stress, and thus for really getting in the mood for Lisbon. It runs a full circle, and offers, for a small price, more than many expensive tours of the city.

The colorful »Eléctricos« follow their roller-coaster run with sudden fun-house turns, until they are jammed together for the night in depots, for example, near the Avenida Duque de Ávila and the Avenida Dona Filipa Vilhena. Another streetcar depot worth seeing is in the Rua 1° de Maio, almost exactly below a concrete column of the »Ponte 25 de Abril«. Careful searching reveals a gorgeous Oldtimer streetcar. How about a »cross-country« ride? This streetcar can be privately rented.

Up and down the streets in the »Eléctrico«

Miradouros

Insights and Outlooks

Up where the »caracol« of »Graça« begins winding downward, the fountain bubbles, a few trees stand, and the streets dead-end on the plateau. The view of the city from here is magnificent: a »Miradouro«, a viewpoint – in this case, the »Miradouro da Graça«. Lisbon is the city of »Miradouros«! These urban clifftop edges are something much better than brilliant city planning or architectonic decoration. For the Lisboans, »Miradouros« mean neighborhood, clubhouse, tavern, playground, lovers' lane, and front yard all in one.

And every »Miradouro« is a pedestal of the soul. Here, from the wrought iron or stone balustrade dividing reality from revery, the Portuguese temperament plunges, lost in thought, into the distance. »Saudade« emerges – that untranslatable, melancholy, typically Portuguese mood. It could express itself thus: »Back there, past the Avenida Almirante Reis, you see the Estremadura. Then, look to the left, the ocean. And on the other shore: Brazil, Rio. Look carefully, amigo.« The province Estremadura stretches north from Lisbon along the Atlantic. Here on the hill at »Largo da Penha da França«, neither ocean nor the Estremaduran landscape are visible. But a »Miradouro« reveals more than the city's silhouette ... The eye gazes over the pitching waves of Lisbon's buildings. They reach to the horizon. The ragged edges of the city are out of sight.

The view of the horizon is omnipresent in Lisbon. It gives wings to the fantasy of a »Lisboeta«. Up on a »Miradouro« with his imaginary vistas, he may easily feel quite close to Rio de Janeiro and São Paulo. For him, Brazil is not as far away as Europe. It was always that way.

A breath of Portuguese-speaking South America floats over Lisbon, only »em Lisboa«, nowhere else in Portugal. The »Praça de São Paulo« – a lively little place. The ancient and beautiful café »A Brasileira« in the Rua Garrett, a bohemian meeting-place. The bookstore »Livraria Brasília« in the Rua da Misericórdia – directly to the right of the Belle Epoque restaurant »Tavares«. Brazilian »Varig« jets thunder over the inner city, day or night. Although the former Portuguese colony, huge Brazil, has long since led its own political life, for Lisbon, Brazil and Rio de Janeiro are understood as part of everyday life: street signs, restaurant names, supermarkets, hairdressers, gambling halls, and large companies express their South American spiritual kinship in the most various ways.

The »Cristo Rei« is also to be seen in this Brazilian context; it is a statue of Jesus over 100 meters high, counting the pedestal. Since the scaffolding came down in 1959, it has served as an inescapable »Miradouro« on the Rio Tejo. The »Cristo Rei« rivals the statue on the Corcovado in Rio de Janeiro. That was the original purpose of its construction: as the embodiment of a bridge between »Lisboa« and Rio. The Jesus monument can be climbed; it stands on a mountain, beyond the sometimes kilometer-wide Rio Tejo, on whose banks the »white city« stretches. Seen from the »Miradouro«-Jesus, »Lisboa« seems very white indeed, especially in contrast to the blue of the water. The Jesus statue triggers associations of »Christian seafaring«. The monumental »Cristo Rei« spreads out his concrete arms over the broadly spanned bridge »Ponte 25 de Abril«, allowing passage for the many container ships, freight steamers, cutters, tugboats, and the white cruise ships that occasionally dock here.

At another spot, one can lose oneself and all thought of time in a maritime view. The stairway across from the harbor entrance at the great swing-bridge (at the »Doca de Alcântara«) connects the Avenida Vinte e Quatro de Julho with the Rua das Janelas Verdes. From up there, where the steps dead-end, Lisbon reveals itself as a harbor city. The distance to the opposite shore of the Tejo seems to shrink to the dimensions of toys in the orange and peach-colored dusk. Seen from here, even the docks and cranes of »Lisnave«, the state shipyards out in Cacilhas, line up next to the »Museu de Arte Antiga« in a dreamy idyll of life and motion, insights and outlooks. Here below the Rua das Janelas Verdes, shipping shows its best side: with the blue-glinting, broad river, the orange/white Tejo ferries (»Cacilheiros«) and the harbor and pier constructions with their characteristic sounds. The »Museu de Arte Antiga« waits next door for visitors. The museum garden offers an unusual view of the low piers. Television antennae all around remind us of everyday life, while noble sculptures stand proudly in this »Miradouro« museum garden. Contemplation has set itself its own monument in these two »Miradouros« in the »Street of Green Windows« (»Janelas Verdes«).

The counterpoint can be found only a few hundred meters to the East. But the way to the »Miradouro de Santa Catarina« is fraught with obstacles. Whoever rides up on the mini-streetcar-»Elevador« (»Ascensor da Bica«) with its step-like seats from the »Valley Station« in a

*»Miradouros« are auto-free playgrounds and peaceful
leisure spots – here at the Rua Santa Catarina*

building entrance to the Rua de São Paulo will, on that terrace viewpoint, have room and opportunity enough to ponder Lisbon's many facets. A petrified, distorted, huge bald head »graces« this location. The monument of the »Adamastor« is a crude sea monstrosity taken from the *Lusíadas* of Luís de Camões and symbolizes the old seamen's fear of the sea. The Portuguese writer imagined the ocean as being so powerful and terrible at the Cape of Good Hope – where the crews 450 years ago had yet to sail to improve trade with India. The little bronze David is missing from the monument. He personified Portuguese sailing lore. David defeated Goliath, the ocean.

Further away, in the villa district »Restelo«, above the stadium, then by foot across the Avenida da Torre de Belém, the view from the chapel sweeps over Lisbon's present and past. Down on the Rio Tejo, the »Torre de Belém« and the cloister complex »Mosteiro dos Jerónimos« bear witness stonily and »Manuelistically« to Portuguese sailing and colonial history. The Tejo broadens out toward the ocean. Every day, the sun seems to sink into the Atlantic halfway between Europe and America … From here, Vasco da Gama, Fernão Magalhães, Pedro Álvares Cabral, and Bartolomeu Dias sailed to discover other worlds for Portugal and to win them for Christendom and for trade.

Similar views heavy with memory wait at the »Miradouro« at the foot of the little chapel »Santo Amaro«, Portugal's first early Renaissance building (1549), whose interior is beautifully decorated with »Azulejos«. Impressive prospects of Lisbon's many faces are also opened up by the lively city park »Jardim da Estrela«. From one of its corners, a hidden path leads up to an elevated vista.

A homey »Miradouro« surprises us on the Rua R.C. Pestana. A road leads through a wrought iron gate, past a spritely fountain and benches, and through plenty of green vegetation to a terraced lookout area with many levels. Hidden in a corner stands the shadowed bust of the prominent Portuguese pianist, Viana da Mota (1868–1948): »Mestre dos Músicos do Seu Tempo« reads the inscription – »the« musician of his time! The »music« up here consists of traffic noise and the slap of cards by neighborhood players. A bench, a sill, or a wall, carefully laid out with a newspaper, serves as card table. When dusk starts to fall, the light of the neon signs on the »Rossio« reflects rhythmically up here, in time with the big city crescendo of heavy traffic and with the turbulence around the »Praça dos Restauradores« and the showcase street »Avenida da Liberdade«.

In Lisbon, the »Miradouro« city, one is almost always looking somewhere down below from somewhere up above. This arrangement with the third dimension also resembles a time machine, because a panorama of the extremely various architectural epochs reveals Lisbon's history as a city. For example, at the hidden »Largo da Academia Nacional de Belas Artes«, the gate to a parking lot opens up an exciting view of the city: of the »Praça do Comércio«, of the Cathedral »Sé«, of the »Castelo de São Jorge«, and even over to the train station and the market halls at the »Cais do Sodré«. Here is a unique and marked impression of Lisbon's development as a city, from the beginnings, through the new beginning after the annihilating earthquake, and up to the present!

The »Miradouro« on the Rua de São Pedro de Alcântara right by the »Mountain Station« of the »Elevador da Gló-

ria« seems like a tiny city park. Sometimes painters try to capture on canvas the scenic fountain on the opposite chain of picturesque hills with the »Castelo«. More photographs are taken here than at almost any other spot. The rampart is inlaid with a stone tablet, chiseled with information orienting one about what seems like a confusedly flowing urban kaleidoscope. To avoid forgetting the details in the overview, follow the downward-winding street below the viewing platform.

Insight into the present of the »Alfacinhas« (=Lisboans) is offered by the »Miradouro« at the »Largo das Necessidades«. The customary »Miradouro« life unfolds itself around the baroque fountain in front of the »Palácio Real das Necessidades«, today's foreign ministry: the neighborhood engaging in small talk, young and old amusing themselves with soccer balls and bicycles, reading newspapers, playing cards, laughing, or necking. Before the »Palácio« was built, a little chapel stood here. There, special prayers were offered for sailors en route to India, and the chapel was named for »Nossa Senhora das Necessidades«. The »good woman« was responsible for the necessary protection of the seafarers. –

The lookout above the valley-like oval, »Alameda D. Afonso Henriques«, that stretches for several hundred meters, shows an entirely different Lisbon. Up there, directly at the Rua Barão de Sabrosa, the eye wins space and looks out over a monumental complex. A cascading fountain arches from the house-high wall at the front end of the broadly sweeping plaza lined with majestic buildings. It is flanked by 13 nude stone women and by rearing horses. When the gigantic basin is filled, it is an astonishing sight. Indirect light is cast on it nights. The spraying waters not only have a monumental effect, they're also called the »Fonte Monumental«. The heavy construction dates from the Salazar period. What a difference to all the other »Miradouros« that make Lisbon so charming …

The way from here to »Graça« completes this »Miradouro« circle. Along the Avenida General Roçadas and, farther below, past the »Miradouro« at the »Largo da Penha da França«, one meets up with the Rua da Graça. There the Calçada do Monte threads its way up to the fantastic »Miradouro da Nossa Senhora do Monte«. It is the most prominent and by far the highest elevation after the »Alfama« mountain. Here one recognizes where one has been before and, at the same time, has an idea of how little one has really seen of Lisbon.

*»Miradouros« surprise with unexpected
panoramas, as here in a view from
the terrace of the »Panteão Nacional«
onto the great basin of the Rio Tejo*

The view from the »Miradouros«, often hidden,
extends beyond the sea of houses
to the distant »Serra de Sintra«

A view into the street canyon toward the »Praça da Figueira« on the edge of the »Baixa« in a quiet hour

59

Big city stress is forgotten at the »Miradouro«
above the cupola of the »Coliseu«

60

Between Today and Yesterday

São Vicente, Azulejos, and São Bento – from Panteão to the Cemitérios

Visually, a giant church appears to dominate the region between »Graça« and the »Alfama«. The »Igreja e Mosteiro de São Vicente« also carries the adjunct »de Fora«, which means »outside«. The complex, given over to its purpose in 1629, was beyond the city walls and outside the legal jurisdiction of the Bishop of Lisbon.

The name comes from »outside« as well. São Vicente is, with Santo António, Lisbon's most famous saint. The legend says that São Vicente, actually a Spaniard, drifted in a ship, dead, around the Ponta de Sagres along the Algarve coast. Two ravens guarded the corpse and navigated Saint Vincent as far as Lisbon. A Spanish king, Philipp II, was so impressed with this that, hundreds of years later during the period of Spanish occupation, he had the church »São Vicente de Fora« built. And this was the ravens' official entry into Lisbon as well.

In the meantime, two ravens and a stylized ship grace the countenance of the city everywhere, whether in the pavement or as »guardians« on almost every streetlamp. Ravens and ship are also the main element of the city coat-of-arms. The historical background of this legend says that the dead body of Vincent was stored in a chapel in Ponta de Sagres, where ravens also nested. After Portugal's founder and first king, Dom Afonso Henriques, had driven away the Moors, he wanted to erect a temple for São Vicente in Lisbon in gratitude for the victory. So he sent a ship on its journey and the »guardian« ravens are supposed to have been along for the ride.

At the corner of »Largo de São Vicente« and Rua Voz do Operário, the road follows the church wall to the »Feira da Ladra«, Lisbon's flea market. The »Feira da Ladra« still draws on the immeasurable resources of the capital of a former worldwide colonial empire, though the jetsam of contemporary civilization stubbornly fends off those relics of the past. There is one thing that can't be found here: stolen goods. The »Feira da Ladra« is persistently translated as »Thieves' Market«. This »ladra«, however, means the chattering, the din, the noise. That is the actual meaning of the word, and it characterizes well this »Uproar Market«. The »Feira da Ladra« is held all around the blindingly white Pantheon on Saturdays and Tuesdays.

Six sarcophagi stand in the Pantheon in memory of Vasco da Gama, Prince Henry the Navigator (Infante D. Henrique), Pedro Álvares Cabral (the discoverer of Brazil), Nuno Álvares Pereira (a warrior), and Afonso de Albuquerque (Viceroy of India). The mortal remains of Luís de Camões, author of the *Lusiads,* allegedly reside in the marble coffer here.

The Pantheon was once the church »Santa Engrácia«, and was built in the style of the Italian Baroque in several stages starting in the 17th century. The building was officially renamed »Grande Panteão Nacional« in 1916, but wasn't dedicated until 1966, when the giant cupola was set on it. –

The Avenida Almirante Reis is lively, many-sided, ever-changing, and always ready with something new to discover. It runs straight as an arrow for many kilometers from the heart of the city up toward the Northeast, toward »Areeiro«, where, yet further North, the newer districts of the city begin.

To the South, at the »Metro« station »Socorro«, the long avenue is still called Rua da Palma. Its name goes back to the story of a German crusader from Bonn. He was among those who died during the reconquest of Lisbon from the Moors. When his bones were reinterred much later in the church »São Vicente de Fora«, a palm grew on the new spot. Whoever touched the palm was healed of all evil. Nowadays, the attempt is being made to give the street a fresher appearance. Between the traffic lanes, trees are being planted, even if they aren't palms.

The Rua da Palma becomes the busy inner city artery and shopping street whose present name is connected with the 1910 revolution. After October 5, 1910, the Portuguese monarchy was a thing of the past. The democratic Republic of Portugal was proclaimed, lived through many vicissitudes, and ended in the dictatorship that emerged in 1928. Carlos Cândido dos Reis, a vice admiral in the navy, had worked for the overthrow of the monarchy. The street bears his name.

The Avenida Almirante Reis officially begins at the »Largo do Intendente Pina Manique« where it conjoins with the Rua da Palma. There, attention is riveted by an angular fountain, built in 1824. A coliseum capable of seating 5,000 people stood on this spot until the end of the last century. It was replaced by the »Coliseu dos Re-of the details are obscured by posters, awnings, neon signs, electric power lines, and streetcar cables.

This Avenida is a street of severe fragmentation, like the gigantic complex, the »Portugália«. The »Azulejos« still evidence the half-ruined brewery from 1913, though the »Cerveja« center now resides in a renovated side wing. One part of the building is renovated; inside, under the wide, vaulted roof of the »Cervejaria Restaurante Portugália«, over a sea-fresh meal of »Marisco«, one takes in the great variety of this Avenida. It includes the night life, a street market in the side streets, and the characteristic metal and glass conservatory facades that cover the rear of a whole building, and upon which the typical iron ladders are affixed; these were the apartments' rear entrances for house servants and deliveries (»Escadas de Serviço«). The Avenida Almirante Reis crosses the »Praça do Chile«, where Lisbon seems to wear the mask of a South American metropolis.

Farther to the East sprawls the huge »Cemitério do Alto de São João«, usually called simply the »Cemitério Oriental« (Eastern Cemetery). It gives the impression of a white city with main and side streets, with mausoleums, little neoclassical temples, and with a great deal of marble decoration. The elevated grounds are steep and seem to fall eastward to the Rio Tejo without any break. Looking to the North, the cemetery buildings seem to complement another city. On a hill, Lisbon's social housing projects are a strong contrast. There, far away on the periphery of the city, the attempt is being made to master the city's housing problems with complex construction programs. –

Lisbon has another such vast cemetery-city. The »Cemetério Ocidental« (Western Cemetery) is better known as »Prazeres« (»Pleasures«) – a scurrilous-seeming epithet. Soon after its opening, it had to be officially forbidden for the next-of-kin to sing and make merry among the gravestones. Before it was transformed into a cemetery, the »Pleasures« plaza had been a place for perfectly normal celebrating.

The two cemeteries, »Oriental« and »Ocidental«, were constructed between 1833 and 1835. Both arose after it was made illegal to bury the dead inside churches. (Many old Portuguese churches still have trap doors in their floors, through which the dead were lowered.) The cemetery »Prazeres« covers 11 hectares (about 27 acres)

The cupola of the »Panteão Nacional« – originally the »Igreja de Santa Engrácia«

creios« (a kind of multi-purpose theater), which is in the Rua das Portas de Santo Antão, in the immediate neighborhood of the »Praça dos Restauradores« and its many excellent restaurants.

The Avenida Almirante Reis, too, resembles a multi-purpose theater, with its many beautiful wrought iron balconies and houses tiled with »Azulejos«, even if some

The »Azulejo« picture shows the victory of
»São Jorge« – »Saint George«, the patron of the
largest castle – over the dragon

– the Eastern Cemetery is larger –, has over 89 streets, some of which are even marked with street signs, and which are often named for native and foreign sculptors and architects. –

To the East, past the »Cemitério Oriental«, one arrives at the impressive church »Madre de Deus«. Because of the earthquake of 1755, only remnants of the Manuelistic facade are left, among them a portal. »Manuelism« was that architectural period in which the medieval seafaring nation Portugal articulated itself in a wealth of nautical motifs. In the interior of »Madre de Deus«, the white-blue »Azulejos« not only tell the life story of São Francisco, parts of the church have been transformed into the national museum for »Azulejos«. It houses many »Azulejo« depictions and its didactic conception has recently been revamped, informing the visitor about the history of the »Azulejos« from their Arabic beginnings up until our own times. »Al zulaich« means »little stones« in Arabic; »Azulejo« has nothing to do with »azul« (Portuguese for »blue«), as is usually falsely claimed, although the »Azulejo« pictures often have blue as their dominating color.

Incidentally, almost all Portuguese words beginning with »al« are of Arabic origin, for example »Algarve« = al gharb = the West. –

The old English double-decker buses commute between the »Madre de Deus« district, named for the church, and the center of the city. They thus present a great opportunity for a long tour of the city as far as the Western end-terminal at the »Palácio da Assembleia Nacional«, at the low price of a normal bus fare. This showcase building is a neoclassical structure, begun in the last century and finished in 1941. The original site of the Portuguese parliament and administration was a Benedictine monastery from the 16th – 17th centuries. The »Palácio de São Bento« was remodelled as the House of Parliament after the dissolution of the Order, and was brought into its present form after a fire destroyed the earlier building that still went under the name of »São Bento«. –

In another direction, the double-decker lines go from »Madre de Deus« out along the long stretches of the piers, which are the real harbor – the »Porto de Lisboa«.

The one-time Senate Hall in the national parliament
»Palácio de São Bento« and the other halls in the
»Assembleia da República« are symbolically protected by
military guards

»Azulejos« – decorative tiles rich in motifs –
originally came to the Iberian Peninsula with the Moors.
In Portugal, this tile artform has been further
developed. Lisbon is worth visiting for these alone –
even the facades of the houses invite visitors

Partial view of the »Palacete dos Viscondes de Sacavém«
in »Madragoa«

66

Even the old »Azulejo« advertisements outlast newer publicity trends

Inconspicuous »Azulejo« advertising can still be found throughout the city

A hidden »Azulejo« depiction of industrial history

Example of typical »Azulejo« facade decoration

*The »Cemitério Oriental« resembles a huge
›white necropolis‹ as much as does
the »Cemitério Ocidental (dos Prazeres)«*

Estufa Fria and King Edward

*The Botanical
Garden and the
Parque Eduardo VII*

Filigree botany and gracious art in the »Estufa Fria«

The »Praça Marquês de Pombal« appears again and again as the downtown pivot point. Standing on a column as a statue 9 meters high, the city-renewer Pombal is visible far and wide. At the foot of the massive shaft of the column, reborn Lisbon, the Reform University in Coimbra, and the political goals of the first government after the earthquake are symbolized. The latter were: efficient agriculture, industrialization, and productive fisheries. These themes are just as relevant today.

In back of the Pombal statue, a broadly divided green area with painstakingly accurately pruned hedges rolls upward, bordered on both sides with tree-lined promenades. This is the »Parque Eduardo VII«, dedicated to the English king who visited Lisbon in 1903. Portugal and Great Britain are old allies. These two countries have the longest and most continuous bilateral relations of any European countries.

In the area around the Northwestern corner of the »Parque Eduardo VII« and at the viewpoint street »Avenida Cardeal Cerejeira«, a mesh of bast matting is conspicuous. Under it, much of the variety of this earth's vegetation thrives in a tropical micro-climate. The »Estufa Fria«, whose iron-and-wood construction was begun in 1930, offers a unique spectacle of nature. The »Estufa Fria« (»Cold Steps«) have been enriched with an Estufa »Quente« (warm) and an Estufa »Doce« (dry). Paths for strolling wander through the »Estufas«, the greenhouses, and continue on outside. Sometimes the »Estufa Fria« serves as an impressively beautiful backdrop for classical music concerts.

A low, hidden building stretches its side wings out on one of the lengths of the »Parque Eduardo VII«. Large-format »Azulejo« pictures gleam on the side facing the park. Infante D. Henrique (Prince Henry the Navigator) looks out over the seas that toss up at him in allegorical form. Another picture shows a galleon sailing over the horizon toward India. The building is the »Pavilhão dos Desportos«, erected in 1932. Since then, the »Pavilion of Sports« has also become a favored arena for oratorical contests in connection with political campaigns.

Revistas and Pastelarias

Amusements and the Appetite for Bolos, Bicas, and Bagaços

Tivoli and »Alegria« sound like fun. »Alegria« means gaiety and is the name of a small plaza on the »Avenida da Liberdade«; »Tivoli« refers to the painstakingly restored cinema, the colorful »Quio$que« (sic!), and the genteel hotel – also on the »Avenida«. But the kind of enjoyments associated with Copenhagen's Tivoli take a different form in Lisbon. Four frosted glass cubes on top of stone columns line the recessed entrance on the »Avenida da Liberdade«. Although the »Parque Mayer« opens up here, these grounds are neither »Park« nor »Tivoli«!

One finds oneself here in the historical center of the Portuguese »Revistas«. These were witty performances that, after 1859, developed into an artform *sui generis*. »Fossilismo e Progresso« was the cunning title of the first Portuguese »Revista«, by Vítor Pavão dos Santos: fossils (in the sense of backwardnesses) and progress. »Revistas« looked back (= revue, review) and attacked social and political evils. They took their cue from the French, who had exported their Paris revues here before 1859. Paradoxically, the »Revistas« in what would become the »Parque Mayer« took inspiration for their increasingly subtle, clever, and amusing texts from the censorship measures of the dying monarchy.

At the same time, hymns – some still very well-known, others not really forgotten – were sung in honor of Lisbon: »Lisboa amada« from 1917 (»Beloved Lisbon«) and »Há festa na Mouraria« (»Celebrating in the Mouraria«) are two of many titles that had their premieres here, as did such »Revista« vocal artists Chaby Pinheiro or Lucinda do Carmo.

These many popular favorites faded before the »Fado«, which made its way onto the revue stages in the »Parque Mayer« as well as in the »Alfama« and in the »Bairro Alto«. Soon a new type of »Fadista«, itself influenced by the »Revistas«, influenced in turn the 100-year-old »Fado de Lisboa«: for example, »Hermínia«, »Amália«, »Amarante«, or »Albertina«. This kind of »Fado« is clearly differentiated from the »Fado« of the university town Coimbra, the only other »Fado« cultivated in Portugal.

Adolfo Mayer, for whom the location is named, was an industrialist. He instigated the renovation of the old theaters grouped around a »Palácio« and in a garden area (»Parque«).

The Rua do Salitre comes here from the »Largo do Rato«. The entire area, including the bordering »Jardim Botânico«, is still referred to colloquially as »Salitre«.

Having a »Bica« in the old café »A Brasileira«

The region now containing the botanical gardens and the »Parque« was called »Salitre« by the Jesuits. Long before the first »Revista«, the first theater, as well as bullfight and circus arenas, established themselves here during the Pombaline era.

This urban ensemble with its gardens, ponds, and terraces was later expanded by Adolfo Mayer to extend, almost like Copenhagen's Tivoli, to the »Plaza of Gaiety« – »Praça de Alegria«. In 1922, it was remodelled again and the theater »Maria Vitória«, still quite popular today, was built. But then pieces of the grounds were repeatedly sliced off for other purposes. Today the »Parque Mayer« is a place with varietés, discotheques, simple amusements – and with a great number of restaurants of widely varying quality.

Literary cabaret, which has found a new home here, is gradually picking up the thread of the cultural inspirations that took their start here and that gave Lisbon and the rest of the country an original and highly refined artform hardly known anywhere outside of Portugal.

Foreign visitors often overlook the »Parque Mayer«. Hardly any European metropole has such a non-touristy and popular attraction right in its center.

Outdoor parties are thrown throughout Lisbon in the summery half of the year. Every June 13th, the round-the-clock spectacle in memory of Santo António draws »Lisboetas« by the thousands into the »Alfama« like a magnet. The permanent amusement park »Feira Popular« also pulls uninterruptedly. From April through October, numerous attractions compete for customers – and delicious smells lure toward countless restaurants. The »Feira Popular« promises gourmet pleasures. Garlands of lights spread out across the clean, tiled, restaurant-lined streets. Carousels, handicraft shops, and even dry goods shops round out the picture. Many fresh groceries are produced here and the typical specialities of other Portuguese provinces are also available.

These other parts of the country, from Madeira to Trásos-Montes, are here at the »Feira Popular« to be wondered at, too; »Portugal Pequenino« is a unique, charming, old-fashioned stage – a kind of miniature of the nation. A complicated pulley system kept this sheet metal and plaster landscape in constant motion long before anyone even imagined plastic or computers.

They are the meeting place for young and old and the whole neighborhood: the Lisboan »Pastelarias«. The prototype boasts big metal-framed window-panes, neon lights, chrome, brass, mirrors, a generously proportioned counter, pastel colors, tiles and »Azulejos« everywhere, a hissing espresso machine, shelves of bottles, ceiling ventilators, and a chest-high glass display case to lean on. The latter is the Pastelaria's heart, with all its »Bolos«, the little cakes: »Jesuitas«, »Xadrês«, »Queques«, »Garibaldis«, »Bolas de Berlim«, »Argentinos«, »Madalenas«, »Mimos«, or »Suspiros«.

And every Pastelaria boasts of its own dreams made of dough and powdered sugar, sometimes with and sometimes without filling.

Nowhere else in Portugal, or perhaps in the world, can a comparable concentration of bakeries be found as is achieved by the characteristic Lisboan »Pastelarias«. They are always a mixture of bakery and bar.

Whether hidden on the little »Largo de Dona Estefânia« with its pretty fountains, or in the »Campo de Ourique« district on the Rua Ferreira Borges with its mighty, walled-in paintings, »Pastelarias« are always places where local color and the art of living paint an authentic picture of Lisbon.

In the West, near the »Mosteiro dos Jerónimos«, inconspicuous letters spell out »Única Fábrica dos Pastéis de Belém«. This »Pastelaria«, more than 150 years old, with its old counter and the luxurious chandeliers, is the original manufacturer of the speciality with the same name; from here, it conquered all of Portugal. But only here can one be sure of getting one's »Pastéis de Belém« served hot. The caramel coating is crisp, dusted with powdered sugar and cinnamon. The »Pastéis« are eaten with a »Bica« – a demitasse of strong espresso – or with a »Bagaço« – fruit brandy.

The oldest Lisboan café, »A Brasileira«, was once a meeting place for authors. It is located in the »Chiado« and exudes a dignified nostalgia. The interior of the »Pastelaria Versailles« in the Avenida da República is as illustrious as the name promises.

In a »Pastelaria«, one needn't remain a stranger for long: »Alfacinhas« are outgoing people. The same is true for encounters in »Restaurantes« and »Tascas«, in »Tascos«, »Cervejarias«, »Ginjinhas«, and in the cafés. Even on a short visit to Lisbon one is sure to make friends – and to find »his« Pastelaria.

But one shouldn't commit oneself too quickly on the restaurant! Lisbon provides so many »Restaurantes« and such a spectrum of menus that a gourmet tour can offer wonderful new surprises every day.

Tea and coffee sales in the »Baixa«

The luxurious café »A Brasileira« in the »Chiado«

Every kind of fresh-caught »Mariscos« are relished.
Guests pick their dinner themselves from rows of live
shrimp, crabs, lobsters, mussels, and other
shellfish in the restaurant windows

*Lisbon's cuisine involves almost innumerable restaurants
for every taste and purse. Guests experience exclusive
dishes and discrete service at the »Restaurante Tavares«,
opened in 1784, in the Rua da Misericórdia*

In »Pastelarias« like this one, the »Pastelaria Versailles«
in the Avenida da República, one meets for a »Bica«, a»Bolo«,
a »Bagaço«, or for a beer

The »Parque Mayer« is a traditional attraction for fans of revue theater, popular entertainment, cabaret, and gourmet delights

The wild cherry liqueur »Ginjinha« remains a great favorite

Retreat from the Past

Avenida da República,
Campo Grande,
Entre Campos, and
Campo Pequeno

After long kilometers, the wide Avenida da República reaches its Southern endpoint at the »Praça Duque de Saldanha«. The monument to the Marechal Duque de Saldanha stands on a column in the middle of the large, circular plaza and thus draws attention to the early 19th century's finally futile efforts to bring the ideas of the French Revolution to Portugal. Seemingly hidden, not far away, is the »Mercado 31 de Janeiro« with its crouching fish hall and the old market halls, clothed to this day with wooden panels.

The city villas on the Avenida da República continue to impress the viewer, although many have been torn down and replaced with concrete structures. Lisbon is less crowded and more clearly laid out here. The cross streets almost always intersect at right angles.

The Rua Alexandre Braga branches off from the cosy little »Jardim Constantino« and reveals typical Lisbon apartment house architecture of the time around 1940.

Farther upward, following the vertical line drawn by the Avenida da República in this part of the city, one arrives at the »Campo Grande«, at the »Big Field«. At the major intersection »Entre Campos«, near the »Feira Popular«, the streets split off to make room in their midst for a restful »green lung« with ponds and many opportunities for entertainment. Remember, however, that airplanes fly at low altitudes over the »Jardim do Campo Grande« toward the nearby Lisbon airport, »Portela de Sacavém«.

The horse racetrack (»Hipódromo«) lies under the landing corridor, and the »Museu de Rafael Bordalo Pinheiro« hides at the Northeastern corner with works by this popular painter and illustrator, who died in 1905. Across from the latter is the pretty »Museu de Cidade«. The development of the city is depicted vividly there. A miniature Lisbon has been erected under glass, showing the city as it was before the earthquake. The »Palácio Pimenta«, which now houses the museum, is the last remaining »Retiro«. Through the 17th century, when this region still lay before the city gates, the inhabitants of the capital liked to come out to the many »Retiros«, where unrestrained parties were given.

To the West, at the »Campo Grande«, the broad »Cidade Universitária« opens out. In the late 1980's, it was connected with the slowly expanding subway net. Some of the newer stations are not merely functional, but architectonic art objects.

The name »Campo Grande« goes back to the time of Portugal's reconquest from the Moors. But at this spot, a royal father-son feud was fought out between Dom Dinis and the future Afonso IV in the year 1323. But the battle on the »Great Guarded Field« never took place. Before that, the area was called »Alvalade-o-Grande«, an Arabian name that finds its complement in »Alvalade-o-Pequeno«, the »Little Guarded Field«. Today, all that remains of this name is »Campo Pequeno«, and the old »Alvalade« is now the district name for a newer Lisbon.

This newer Lisbon is the result of the expansion of the city in the 1940's. During World War II, when other countries couldn't begin to think of intensive expansion of their cities, Lisbon systematically extended itself – the only large European city to do so. The plans for »Alvalade« originated with the Portuguese city-planner Faria da Costa in 1935. On an area of 230 hectares, or about 570 acres, an »Urbanização« arose, like the suburbs or satellite towns that grew decades later in the rest of Europe: a residential area with planned shops, cinemas, banks, cafés, and offices, comparable with such social and educational institutions as the »Hospital de Santa Maria« and the »Instituto Superior Técnico«.

In contrast to the rest of Lisbon, the geometry of this development seems rather cool. One can certainly still make out the architectural philosophy that was a part of the »Estado Novo«. The regime then current had abbreviated its ideology in this title, »New State«. But in streets like the Avenida de Roma, today's »Praça Dr. Francisco Sá Carneiro«, or the »Praça de Londres«, Lusitanian vitality has long since moved in, and a lot of green vegetation has grown up everywhere.

With the broad Avenida dos Estados Unidos da América, the attempt was made to visually approximate the architecture of the larger cities of the United States. A great many »Lisboetas« doubt that this was such a good idea.

In any case, the complex project of systematically grafting the many-sided urbane life onto the outskirts of the city was first practiced on a grand scale in Lisbon. Later, this trend was the great fashion for a long time in the rest of Europe. In addition to the Avenidas de Roma and dos Estados Unidos da América, the bustling Avenida da Igreja and the main thoroughfare Avenida do Brasil characterize this portion of the newer Lisbon. In our time, the architectural signature of Tomás Taveira has begun to draw a completely different profile of the city.

One of the many characteristic buildings from the »Estado Novo« period

It is impossible to overlook the large, round, red building standing in the middle of the »Campo Pequeno« with its little tower and a central cupola in clearly Arabian style and with its windows so reminiscent of a seraglio. This is Lisbon's only bullfighting stadium, the »Praça de Touros«, dedicated in 1882. When the »Campo Pequeno« is spoken of today, this place for »espectáculos tauromáticos« is meant.

Before the bullfights were moved here to this probably most well-respected »Praça dos Touros« in Portugal, they were staged – since 1647 – on the »Rossio« (where the Inquisition palace stood and carried out bloody executions at the present day location of the »Teatro Nacional Dona Maria II«) and – after 1687 – on the »Terreiro do Paço« (today's »Praça do Comércio«). But the first bullfighting arena was erected in »Belém«, and Portugal's first permanent, ring-shaped arena for bullfights was built in »Salitre« (now the »Parque Mayer«). Professional »Toureiros« are known within Portugal since the middle of the last century. The first were Spanish matadors working under contract.

In Lisbon, the bullfighting season generally begins on Easter Sunday and continues into the autumn.

Attacking the bull from horseback plays a much greater role in Portugal than in Spain and the Latin American countries. This tradition is rooted in the history of the cavalry. The »Cavaleiro« often rides in the high formal style. And, as is well known, in Portugal the bull does not die in the arena, as he does in Spain. This kind of public slaughtering of the animals was outlawed during the 18th century. Instead, the goal is to »humiliate« the black bruiser. In the »pega à portuguesa«, the bull is approached without weapons in the attempt to grasp him by the horns and throw him to the ground.

The high points of the »corridas« in the »Praça de Touros« are the gala historical performances. All of the participants are vested in old costumes; horse carriages rattle up; and brass bands play. The series of up to eight bullfights is more a colorful show than a particularly bloody spectacle.

The steer and the »Toureiro« stand
eye-to-eye. In the last phase of every bullfight,
the »Toureiro« must ›take the bull by the horns‹
and defeat him only with muscle power
and the help of the »Forcados«

86

The »Praça de Touros« on the »Campo Pequeno«
is Portugal's most important arena and houses
a bullfighting museum in its towers.
In Portuguese bullfights,
the animals are not killed

One of the typical city villas in the area around the Avenida
Fontes Pereira de Melo and the Avenida da República.
Structures like these are increasingly being replaced by
new architecture

Panorama with Memories

Estrela, Lapa, and Campo de Ourique

The »Jardim da Estrela«, always green and a good 100 years old, exudes a quiet friendliness. In the cooler seasons, the »Lisboetas« are sun-starved, too, and move their chairs out of the shade on the »Esplanada«. In the middle of the park, a painstakingly restored, finely filigreed iron »Coreto« rises. Hardly any park between the Algarve coast and the province of Trás-os-Montes does without a »Coreto«. Sometimes these pavilions serve as a dance floor, sometimes as an umbrella, sometimes as a meeting place, sometimes as a playground – but, above all, they are used by bands during the many »Festas« and »Romarias«.

The »Basílica da Estrela« in front of the park gates is one of the visual and architectural highlights of Lisbon. After eleven years of construction work begun in 1779, the two architects Mateus Vicente and Reinaldo Manuel had completed a work important for another reason as well. The two architects were Ludovice's last students. That was the German named Ludwig who designed the Mafra Convent. The »Basílica da Estrela« is therefore seen as the architectural heir of the Mafra Convent, for the attempt had been made to apply here the lessons learned from mistakes made there. Behind the towers on the front, a high white cupola vaults over the »ship« of the church. In it, a stroll with a panoramic view is sometimes permitted.

From the rooftop terrace of the »Casa dos Açores« in the Rua dos Navegantes, one's glance turns again to the broad blue band connecting the Rio Tejo with the Atlantic, and toward »Madragoa« as well.

This district of the city was once the home of the fish women, the »varinas«. They often came from the Northern Portuguese port Ovar, which also explains the etymology of their name. The »varinas« or »vareiras«, with their baskets on their heads, are now found only in the market halls on the »Cais do Sodré«. For a long time, they have come from elsewhere, often from Africa.

The Rua do Sacramento à Lapa leads past the former »Palacete dos Viscondes de Sacavém«. The sober facade of this building is enriched around the windows with playful, variegated ceramic decorations, the like of which are to be found in no other Lisboan streets. This street crosses »Madragoa« like an axis. The name comes from a »Casa das Madres« (Madre = Mother, or Abbess) in Goa, a former Portuguese colony in India.

The district of »Lapa« complements this quarter. The palatial city villas, often hiding behind high walls and lush vegetation, indicate the exclusivity of the area. »Lapa« is a favorite address for diplomatic missions. The English started the fashion in the 19th century, isolating themselves from everyday life in Lisbon. The former »Negro Quarter«, which was called »Mocambo« in the 17th and 18th centuries, was, in time, subjected not only to a change of name, but also to a social restructuring. As it became more attractive to them, the Portuguese aristocracy followed the British into »Lapa«, and were followed in turn by the upper middle class, and today many embassies are located here.

Interesting roads lead back downtown. The Rua de S. Domingos à Lapa almost meets the Rua das Janelas Verdes near the »Museu de Arte Antiga«, which houses »The Temptations of Saint Anthony« by Hieronymus Bosch, as well as many other art treasures.

From the »Museu de Arte Antiga« or from the Calçada da Estrela, one can ride downtown with the »Eléctricos«, uphill and downhill, through extremely lively districts. –

One way leading downtown from »Madragoa« through »Estrela« brushes »Campo de Ourique«. This district has its own calm character. A different rhythm seems to pulse in the tree-lined avenues like the Rua Ferreira Borges.

But beforehand, in the little Rua do Patrocínio at the border to »Estrela«, every pulse is interrupted. Deep stillness rules behind an inconspicuous wall. The tombstones, jammed into a tiny cemetery, read »Hier ruht …«: »Here lies …« in German. The plots show the names of German families who have long lived here. The obscure and hidden »Cemitério Alemão« is the only German cemetery in Portugal – as unique as the English cemetery in the Rua São Jorge or its neighbor, the Jewish cemetery.

In »Campo de Ourique«, the past lives on in the present. The name of the district recalls the battle between the armies of Dom Afonso Henriques and the Moors in the little town of Ourique in the province »Alentejo«, on July 25, 1139.

Another typical, enjoyable little park is fit into the rectangular street corner at the Rua Quatro de Infantaria: the »Jardim da Parada«. Maria da Fonte stands there as a small white monument, charging with a pistol in her hand to fight, apparently, for her rights. In a certain way, Maria da Fonte was perhaps the first Portuguese women's-rights advocate. She was the leader of an agrarian

The old German cemetery lies behind a high wall

revolt in 1846, in which many women participated. The revolt spread from Póvoa de Lanhoso in the province Minho, and was directed against reform plans of the then-current government.

Progress manifests itself in a different way in this district. Many buildings were constructed right after the earthquake in the 18th century. The structures and those courtyards still intact continue to set standards today. This region in the vicinity of the Rua Ferreira Borges with its checkerboard-patterned streets resembles the better-known »Baixa«. A second »Cidade Pombalina« has emerged here, too, still almost unnoticed. This was also the area of the »Panificação«: bread production was concentrated here, together with plenty of sweets. These reminiscences of the past and their connections with the present can be called up in the pastelaria »A Tentadora« (»Temptation«), with its lush Art Nouveau facade.

The white »Basílica da Estrela« across from the beautiful »Jardim da Estrela«

From the Docks to the Discoverers

Alcântara, Belém, Restelo

The Calçada do Livramento leads to the »Miradouro« in front of the »Palácio Real das Necessidades«, the current foreign ministry. This »Miradouro« offers a wide view of the harbor facilities and of the ships in »Alcântara«.

The district is a workers' district and stretches along the Rio Tejo. The »Porto de Lisboa« is continued in the harbor basin of the »Doca de Alcântara«. Along Lisbon's 15 kilometers of piers, freight ships from all over the world dock beside occasional giant cruise ships and almost always beside some large sailing boat from faraway.

»Alcântara« is a word borrowed from Arabic and means »stone bridge«. There were quite a few of them here until the earthquake of 1775 destroyed them and changed the line of the shore. »Alcântara« became the new home for many of the victims of the catastrophe. The newly emerging harbor district was also the cradle of Portuguese industrialization. The Marquês de Pombal founded special training centers, the »Escolas Industriais«. With industrialization, social problems arose similar to those found in the great industrial nations, if smaller in extent. But Portugal had prepared earlier than other countries. Queen Maria Pia opened the first orphanages, and around the turn of the 18th to the 19th century, Queen Dona Amélia opened the country's first department of health in »Alcântara«. Later, people suffering from lung disease were treated here.

»Alcântara« has retained the character given it by work and workers.

Across from the tapering steel bridge, across the »Marginal« and the City Train, a building from the 1940's spreads itself out. It is the »Gare Marítima de Alcântara«. Inside, huge wall murals stretch upward on the walls of the lofty hall. The then-current authoritarian regime had called upon the country's artists to fill the walls with works in a style of »Portuguese Realism«. These heroizing portrayals are usually far from the public eye, but the »Gare Marítima de Alcântara« achieved a sad fame in Portugal. Until April 25, 1974, the day when, in the »Carnation Revolution«, the democratic restructuring of the country began, this was called – in whispers – the »Palace of Tears«. Here, families parted from their sons and fathers when the men were shipped out to serve as soldiers in the colonial wars overseas. –

The high white monument commemorating Portuguese voyages of discovery throughout the world comes into view – »Padrão dos Descobrimentos«. It towers amid the basins of the yacht harbor. The monument shows the stylized bow of a sailing ship, flanked by numerous persons connected with this period of Portuguese history, who are being led by Prince Henry the Navigator. From the viewing platform high above, one recognizes a giant compass at the foot of the »Discoverers Monument«. It symbolizes and characterizes Portugal's »Discoverer Nature«. This broad mosaic compass was a present from the Republic of South Africa to the Portuguese State in honor of the 500th anniversary of the death of Prince Henry, the Infante D. Henrique.

On the way to the »Torre de Belém«, one immediately comes upon one of the few remaining reminders of »Manuelism«. In the form of petrified anchors, starfish, mussels, rigging, and other maritime paraphernalia, King Manuel I's architectural and decorative efforts to immortalize the »Golden Age« of Portugal's sea power were very popular throughout the country.

The »Torre de Belém« was planned as a bulwark and was built on an island in the Rio Tejo at the beginning of the 16th century. The face of this impressive construction is turned toward the water, not the land where the tower stands. The earthquake changed the course of the river, but spared what is now the »Belém« (»Bethlehem«) district as well as the »Torre«.

Napoleon's troops came in 1807 and dismantled the upper storeys of the defense installation. The French were later driven off, the Portuguese court returned from its Brazilian exile, the missing storeys were rebuilt onto the »Torre de Belém«, and, since 1985, it displays itself as a fully restored structure in the best condition it has ever been in.

At night, lights are trained on this pale, cubical building that stands like a beacon recalling Portugal's colonial past – recalling the dark accompaniments of the discoveries as well as the great seafaring achievements. –

Fountains attract the visitor to the broadly laid out »Mosteiro dos Jerónimos«. The monastery of the former Hieronymus Order is one of Lisbon's most spectacular pieces of architecture. The two-storey cloister is an impressive, Manuelistic stone document of the period. History tells us that King Manuel I took an oath to have such a monastery built if Captain Vasco da Gama reached and returned from India. The seafarer was successful. Three years after his return, in 1502, about 70 years of construction on the »Mosteiro dos Jerónimos« began. But instead of Vasco da Gama, the statue of Prince Henry the

Navigator graces the entrance portal – he is regarded as the »spiritual father« of all Portuguese seamen.

The »Mosteiro dos Jerónimos« survived the great earthquake. In the 19th century, the religious order was dissolved; the patron saint – a translator of the Bible and Church teacher – had been immortalized much earlier by Albrecht Dürer in several engravings of Hieronymus. Dürer brought an indirect touch of world fame to the cloister complex in another way as well. In 1515, the forecourt of the »Mosteiro«, where the fountains nowspray, was supposed to provide the setting for an unusual prizefight. Dom Manuel I and many »Lisboetas« wanted to know which was the mightiest animal on earth, the elephant or the rhinoceros. One specimen of each species was shipped to Lisbon. Until then, no specimen of either animal was known firsthand anywhere in Europe. The elephant is supposed to have fled at the sight of the snorting rhinoceros. The involuntary victor, the rhinoceros, was supposed to be given to Pope Gregory XII as a present. The sea voyage to Rome came to a premature end when the thick-skinned animal drowned. Albrecht Dürer took the role of chronicler and made a woodcut of the prominent beast. The »1515 Rhinoceros A.D.« – »Das ist hie mit all seiner gestalt Abconterfeit…« (»This is here with his entire form reproduced…«) – has kept its fame down to the present day.

In Lisbon, the city with well over two dozen important museums, archives, and libraries – from the famous and spaciously divided »Fundação Calouste Gulbenkian« on the »Praça da Espanha« to the obscure little postal museum in the Rua de Dona Estefânia – many of these cultural institutions are grouped around the »Mosteiro dos Jerónimos«. The most popular is the Coach Museum, which presents the world's largest collection of its kind in a side wing of the »Palácio de Belém« – splendid, odd, and technically fascinating vehicles. To the side of the cloister, next to the planetarium of the »Gulbenkian« foundation, the »Museu da Marinha« exhibits maritime showpieces from all periods in history. The »Museu Nacional de Arqueologia e Etnologia« and the »Museu de Arte Popular«, with its typical examples of folk art from the Portuguese provinces, are in the neighborhood. The »Museu da Electricidade« is intended to contain objects of more recent vintage. The most lively museum of all is the »Jardim do Ultramar/Jardim Botânico de Belém«, planted by the Marquês de Pombal. The great variety of vegetation seems to transport the visitor to other continents.

The unfinished »Palácio da Ajuda«, the last royal palace was erected, complete with royal furnishings, on the top of a hill. Today, diplomatic receptions are held there. The excellent library was installed, again, by Pombal. An entirely different sort of museum is found in the intimate »Páteo Alfacinha« in the Rua do Guarda-Jóias. Here, a young little artificial village has arisen, authentically housing every detail of Lisbon's architectural history – from small shops to facade decorations. The »Páteo Alfacinha« provides a stately backdrop for diverse events, including political gatherings.

»Belém« has grown to be synonymous with political administration and maneuvering. The President resides in the »Palácio de Belém«. –

Every evening, when the sun sinks into the sea and the evening star rises over Bethlehem, i.e. »Belém«, and over the elevated, idyllic »Miradouro« at the »Capela dos Jerónimos«, Lisbon displays itself as the most beautiful mountainous seaport. Up here, »Belém« blends into the noble villa district »Restelo«.

The huge »Estádio Municipal do Restelo« is the home turf of the soccer club »O Belenenses«. It is true that Lisbon's more important soccer teams have their stadiums elsewhere, like the »Sporting Clube de Portugal« North of the »Campo Grande« or »Sport Lisboa e Benfica« in the giant oval by the Northern Bypass Highway. But the stadium in »Restelo« is still Lisbon's only open air stage for rock concerts and other spectacles. The nearest other place where this kind of event can take place is the bullfighting arena in the distant suburb Cascais.

»Restelo« boasts Lisbon's only windmills. The two well-kept »Moínhos de Santana« are foreign even to many experts on the city. All the better known is the »Parque do Restelo«, though it isn't nearly as well-liked, for on this large plaza (»Parque«), the police tow away many of the illegal parkers of this city, notorious for its shortage of parking places.

The »Torre de Belém« is one of the most impressive
structural monuments from Portugal's ›Golden Century‹

*The compass at the »Padrão dos Descobrimentos« points
out the ocean voyages of the Portuguese discoverers*

*The elongated facade of the »Mosteiro dos Jerónimos«
is free of all bombastic decoration and ends in pointed
spires. One's glance is directed to the elaborately
styled portals*

*Style elements of ›Manuelism‹
are to be found everywhere in the great
»Mosteiro dos Jerónimos«. The former
cloister survived the earthquake of 1755*

*A »Barco Moliceiro de Aveiro« in the huge and
comprehensive marine museum*

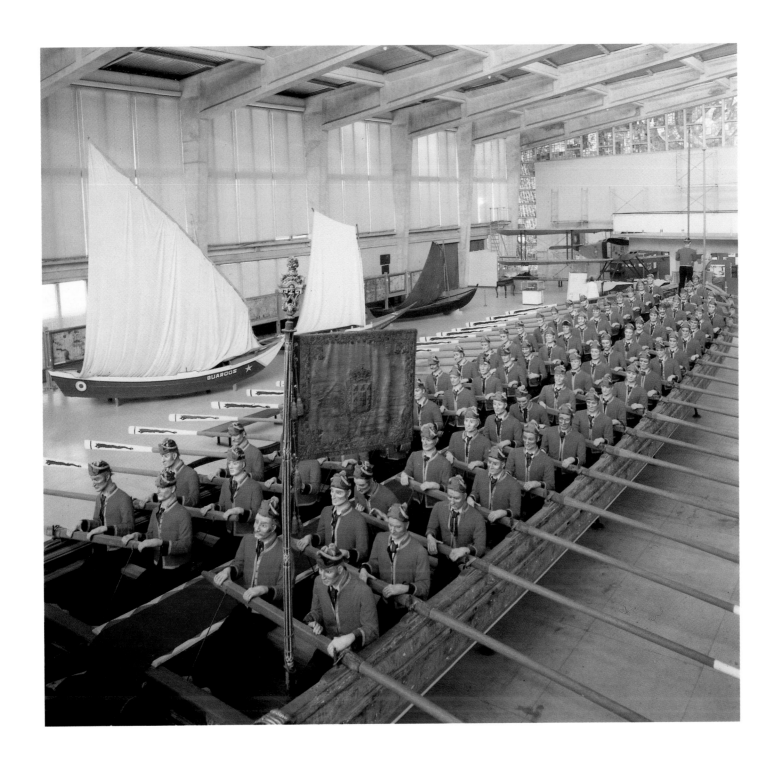

*The »Museu da Marinha« and its exhibits, like these royal »Bergantim Real«,
are housed in the »Mosteiro dos Jerónimos«*

The famous Coach Museum in the »Belém« district

Hill and Vale

*Monsanto and the
Aqueduto das Águas
Livres*

The »Parque Florestal de Monsanto« climbs to a maximum height of 215 meters. The map of the city shows a great green region taking up about a quarter of the incorporated area of Lisbon. The grounds are cut by the highway toward Sintra and Cascais. Lisbon's most important »Parque de Campismo« spreads on the slopes. The peaks of the hills, for example the »Panorâmico« restaurant or »Miradouro de Montes Claros«, offer wide vistas – as does the »Forte de Monsanto«. From this installation, Lisbon shows another side of itself – far and wide, no water. Instead, the Northwestern residential areas move into view.

Far below in »Sete Rios«, the »Jardim Zoológico« opens its gates. The trains move in a great arc from the »Rossio« station around »Monsanto« en route to the noble destination Sintra. The station »S. Domingos« is the best stop on the line for those who want to experience the effects of the modern new building developments. »S. Domingos« has direct connections to »Monsanto«.

Long ago, the hilly region was reforested, and now it is a tangled togetherness of nature and streets, traffic, villas and simple housing, of forests, viewpoint restaurants, antennas, the Court of Law and a ceramics factory. Campers still encounter herds of sheep and find broad plateaus.

To the Northeast, in the »Bairro da Serafina«, one stumbles upon the arcades of a grandiose construction: parts of the »Aqueduto das Águas Livres«. The aqueduct is stretched high and broadly past »Campolide« into the outer district of »Campo de Ourique« and ends near the »Largo do Rato« at the cosy »Jardim de Amoreiras«. The »end-terminal« of the aqueduct is in the building of the »Mãe-de-Água«. This »Mother of the Water« is not only an industrial monument in the history of water management (5500 cubic meters volume), it now also serves as a setting for concerts, providing plenty of atmosphere. From here, the gaze follows the huge water line. It is about 20 kilometers long and begins at the bubbling springs in Belas. They were the source of the name for the »Aqueduto das Águas Livres« – the »aqueduct of free-flowing water«. The aqueduct took over 100 years to build (1732–1834), sometimes underground, sometimes over the 109 more or less visible archways. The angle of descent is constant, and, since the topography exhibits an extemely various profile, this water line is invisible for over 4650 meters. On these stretches – for example, in Benfica near the wagon factory – it can only be found by those who know the locality well, while elsewhere it towers as a giant aqueduct.

Over a distance of 941 meters, 21 round and 14 pointed arches connect »Monsanto« with the inner city, right across the »Alcântara« valley and the highway intersections. The large arch over the Avenida Calouste Gulbenkian is 58 meters high and 24 meters wide.

Plans to provide arid Lisbon with fresh water were made very early. The lack of wholesome water and the associated unhygienic living conditions caused terrible epidemics in Lisbon much more frequently than in many other cities. The majestic and rich metropolis was also a stinking and water-impoverished one! Dom João V finally followed up old insights with planned action, providing the city with a constant supply of fresh water as early as 1748, 86 years before the »Aqueduto das Águas Livres« was finally completed. The earthquake of 1755 had been unable to destroy the aqueduct; otherwise the city and its inhabitants would have been in much direr straits than they were already. And even the city's renewer, the Marquês de Pombal, would have asked himself whether Lisbon could have been saved at all!

Farmers in such surrounding areas as Benfica – known today for the soccer team – used the »Aqueduto« as a convenient means of transporting produce to the markets in »Alcântara«. With filled wallets, they took the same way over the aqueduct on their return, a fact that was soon known to many highwaymen. Robberies became more frequent and when, in addition, the first suicides sprung from the aqueduct, passage was closed to the public. That was 1852. Not until 1986 did the »Câmara Municipal de Lisboa« decide to reopen the »Aqueduto das Águas Livres« for beautiful and – now – safe strolling: to the Northeast lies the »Praça de Espanha« with Portugal's most important cultural institution, the »Fundação Calouste Gulbenkian«. This stands in an ideal relationship diagonally across the aqueduct with the museums in »Belém«. In the depths around the supporting arches, highways distribute traffic eastward into the turbulent inner city and westward into the quieter outskirts.

Way up in the »Parque Florestal de Monsanto«, modern restaurants beckon with magnificent views of the city

The »Aqueduto das Águas Livres« connects »Monsanto«
with the downtown area across the »Alcântara« valley

The Southern Edge of the City

A Ponte, Cacilhas, and Cristo Rei

Two traffic lanes in each direction, suspended 70 meters above the river from two 190 meter high masts, lead for more than a kilometer across the Rio Tejo. The foundations of these gigantic bridge masts reach down 82 meters under the river bed. The suspension bridge measures 2278 meters in its entirety. It was dedicated in 1966 after a four-year construction phase, and carries the official name of »Ponte 25 de Abril« – the date of the 1974 revolution. Colloquially, it is generally called simply »a Ponte«, »the bridge«. It is an American construction.

From a distance, the narrow band of its roadway makes the impression of an artificial Lisboan horizon. It stretches from the »Belém« district to »Cacilhas« and »Almada« on the opposite Tejo shore. On the Lisbon side, the street winds its way from the »Largo de Alcântara« up to the bridge, for the opposite bridgehead is embedded high up in a chain of hills.

»A Ponte« connects the greater metropolitan area of the capital with the country's South. It is far and wide the only bridge over the Rio Tejo, which divides Lisbon's Northern coastal area from the interior – and the bridge is simultaneously Lisbon's most impressive »Miradouro«. Coming from the South, the highway follows the Rio Tejo up to the chain of hills, not revealing any view of the »White City« until directly before the bridge entrance.

Innumerable electric lamps are attached to the steel cables gracefully curving between the masts and the shores. When the lights are turned on at night, they remind one of the silhouettes of two circus tents pitched next to each other.

The bridge is visible – and very audible! For its entire length over the water, the bridge's inner traffic lanes consist of metal bars; the rolling tires of the cars create a dissonant concert that can be heard quite far away. –

Almada and Cacilhas blend into each other. These Lisboan suburbs and outlying industrial areas are located on the Arrábida Peninsula. In Cacilhas, the docks of the huge shipyard »Lisnave« line the street. Many Lisboans take the »Cacilheiros«, the ferry boats, from »Terreiro do Paço« or from »Cais do Sodré« across to their jobs – or from there to the capital. Car drivers rumble over swaying gangways to be waved onto the car ferries. The »ocean cruise« may only go across the Rio Tejo, but on board the »Cacilheiros« one believes Lisbon to be directly on the seacoast. The city gleams white across the river to Cacilhas. The ferry isn't even hitched yet

Two ravens accompany a boat containing the body of the martyr »São Vicente« from the »Algarve« coast to Lisbon. This emblem of the city appears everywhere – in the street pavement, on street lamps, as a relief, or in the form of a small metal sculpture

before the passengers start springing from its edge to the pier wall.

The small Old City core of Cacilhas is famous for its simple but outstanding seafood restaurants. They wait, one after the other, in the immediate vicinity of the ferry dock.

Beyond Cacilhas, driving toward Almada, a road branches off, leading way up to the plateau on which the »Cristo Rei« stands. This monument, dedicated in 1959 and visible for a great distance, stands on a 110 meter high mountain and an angular, 82 meter high pedestal, and then stretches another 28 meters upwards.

High above the terrace, the statue of Jesus spreads its arms. An elevator within the pedestal takes one to the terrace. Although the »Cristo Rei« is easily seen from almost everywhere, it is much harder to actually find one's way to it. The concrete monument is the most massive of Lisbon's viewpoints and views – comparable to the Jesus statue on the Corcovado in Rio de Janeiro. The association is no coincidence; this effect was planned by the city fathers at the time.

The statue of »Cristo Rei« across from the harbor facilities

The mighty »Ponte 25 de Abril« across the Rio Tejo and the little sailing ship of Bartolomeu Dias – as if the legendary captain were setting off again on the long sea route to the Cape of Good Hope

Last Station: Cascais

With the City Train to America

From the »Praça Marquês de Pombal«, one quickly reaches the highway leading straight through the »Parque Florestal de Monsanto« to the Northwestern suburbs. The Western area can be reached by way of the highway as well as over the long arterial street that begins on the »Praça do Comércio« and ends in Estoril or Cascais. While this thoroughfare frequently changes its name underway, it is generally known as the »Estrada Marginal«. It stretches as far as Cascais, 25 kilometers away by road, always within sight of the Rio Tejo or the Atlantic Ocean. During rush hour, traffic regularly comes to a standstill, and the drive can last for ever.

Estoril, Monte Estoril, and Cascais are upper class suburbs. They long ago grew together into one city, and it in turn with Lisbon, to which, however, they are not administratively tied. An elegant express bus line connects Cascais with downtown Lisbon.

But the optimal mode of transportation is the city train. It provides an interesting trip that goes »almost to America«. A ride on the city train is almost like a sea cruise. It goes constantly beside the water, with hardly any interruptions – first along the Rio Tejo, then beside the Atlantic. Particularly foamy waves may even spray through opened doors into the cars.

A fortress-like beacon, the »Bugio«, rests in front of a white sandbank in the middle of the Rio Tejo's kilometer-wide mouth, thus dividing the Rio Tejo into two channels, the »Barra Grande« and the »Barra Pequena«.

The city train ride begins at the city end-terminal at the »Cais do Sodré«. There, many streets cross the rails. A signalman stands next to the barrier at each crossing. By hand, he – or she – signals »Go« with a green flag to the oncoming city train engineer. The journey leads past the stations »Alcântara« and »Belém«, past the »Mosteiro dos Jerónimos«, past the discoverer's monument and the »Torre de Belém« as far as Cascais, where the »Linha« has its end.

On the way, it makes its stops, for example in »Dafundo«. There the legendary seafarer Vasco da Gama has given his name to a restored aquarium with as much age as it has style, and of course a notable oceanographic collection.

At the station »Oeiras«, about 10 kilometers from the »Cais do Sodré«, the journey along the Rio Tejo ends. The shoreline and the rail line bend toward the ocean and continue on the »Costa do Sol«. The name »Coast of the Sun« is apt for this stretch of the Lisboan Atlantic coast.

One can stop in »Oeiras« to pay a visit to the »Palácio Marquês de Pombal«. The most famous Portuguese of modern times lived in this noble edifice surrounded by a park. Perhaps the idea for the »Baixa Pombalina« was born here.

Continuing to follow the »Costa do Sol«, the »Linha« bends once more, allowing travellers to detrain at the beach town »Carcavelos«. It is already the wide Atlantic that crashes on these shores. Far beyond the horizon lies America. The New World stands in a particular relationship to »Carcavelos«, because, on the 27th of August, 1893, a technical achievement of international importance was celebrated: the continental endpoint of an undersea cable connecting the Azores and the mainland was built here. This Portuguese archipelago in the Atlantic lies about halfway between Europe and America, and has a long history as way-station between the Old World and the New World. When the laying of the Transatlantic Cable connected the Azores with America, a continuous communication line from the one continent to the other had been achieved. –

The city train passes bastions and forts spaced evenly along the shoreline. These defense installations on the Rio Tejo and Atlantic, 17 in all, are mighty architectural monuments, mostly from the period when the Spanish ruled over Portugal (1580–1640). They were intended to protect the city and its harbors from unwanted visits by foreign fleets. Today, these former defenses are either in private or in military hand; some serve as fancy restaurants, as a hotel, or as a stately mansion.

The rest of the trip to Cascais goes past suburban train stations and, again and again, beaches. In genteel Estoril, the city train stops directly at the »Tamariz« beach, which has direct access to the station.

In Estoril, the eyes are ineluctably drawn to the lordly mansions as well as to the broad, well-kept park. The latter stretches as far as the »Casino«, Portugal's most worldly establishment of its kind. In addition to gambling salons, the building also contains rooms for banquets and cultural activities – up to and including revue and extravaganza. –

Two city train stations further, the journey in silvery-gleaming aluminum cars ends in Cascais. Whoever considers himself someone special lives in this former sleepy fishing village: artists, businessmen, the upper crust, and the rich, also politicians and many foreigners. But that is Cascais, too: the place is socially well-mixed.

The bay of »Cascais« and a view toward »Estoril«

The »normal« Portuguese dominate the town visually – except in summer, when so many tourists populate this beautifully located Lisbon suburb.

The breakwater and the shore road on the main bay of Cascais were almost completely destroyed by heavy storms in 1984. So the beach, the pier, and the pedestrian area were laid out anew. Pedestrian paths cross the jammed main street. Even in winter, domestic and foreign visitors crowd the passages barred to autos. In the weeks around Christmas, Cascais radiates with the glory of numerous garlands of electric lights hung over the alleys.

The coast road parallels a daily open air market and leads past the »Boca do Inferno«, the »Mouth of Hell«, where a huge hollow in the rocks has been washed out by the Atlantic's roaring, threatening waves.

*Far from the shoreline in the wide region of the
Atlantic mouth of the Rio Tejo, the beacon
island »Bugio« greets international shipping
on its way to and from Lisbon*

On the
Cabo da Roca

Where Europe Starts

The Atlantic between the »Guincho« and the »Cabo da Roca«

The »Lisbon Coast« bends sharply northward, increasing in natural beauty with every meter. The dune landscape has been declared a national preserve. There is an occasional restaurant, some built right into the cliffs. The waves of the Atlantic break in meter-high cascades of foam along the increasingly steep coast. Sport fishermen make good catches from the cliffs. Bathers sun themselves on the »Guincho« beach. On this broad semi-circle, the constant wind drives little sand dunes before it and often over the roadway. It seems as if a desert had been blown into the sea. At the uncrowded »Guincho« beach and its surroundings, one finally finds oneself at the thundering Atlantic. The proximity to Lisbon is soon forgotten, and, in the summer, going for a swim in the ocean refreshes wonderfully from the heat of the city. –

The coast road, leading directly out of the center of the city about 35 kilometers away, rises in wide curves up into the »Serra de Sintra« as far as barren »Cabo da Roca«. There Lisbon »ends«, although the official boundary was crossed long ago.

Seen from this high, harsh cape, the horizon magnificently divides the sky and the ocean with a straight and infinite line. Little cloud banks camp in front of the sun in apparently unreachable distance. How far might they be? Portuguese explorers and traders may have asked the same question half a millenium ago. Dusk spreads intoxicating rainbow colors over the Atlantic. High above the nearby lighthouse, a reflector with a diameter of six meters throws its signals far across the ocean and the coast.

Certificates are awarded in the neighboring restaurant. They confirm that one has visited Europe's westernmost tip. Here ends the »R.N. – Rodoviária Nacional« bus system, which connects the city train station with the »Cabo da Roca«.

Here, too, ends Europe. From the deeply falling cliffs beside the lighthouse, the Occident's westernmost fingers break off abruptly into the Atlantic.

Far, far away, America emerges again – greeted by the European seafarers as the »New World«.

Majestic

In the Serra de Sintra, in Queluz and the Mafra Convent

The »Serra de Sintra« is Lisbon's »house« mountain range – and also a climate divider. Its up to 530 meter high peaks are often veiled in fog. The »Serra« has a climate of its own; it is moister, fresher, and, in the summer, cooler than the plains.

The most important town is Sintra, whose name traditionally stands for the history of and for many stories about the Portuguese monarchy. Dom João I was the founder of the second monarchic dynasty, which supplanted the Burgundian era in the 14th century. From then on, the »Aviz« conducted their government business not only from Lisbon, but also from the summer residences in Sintra. This custom was followed until the end of the Portuguese monarchy in the year 1910, and even today the palaces and dignified edifices provide the setting for many spectacular social events.

The sea and colonial power Portugal revelled for about 150 years in the »Golden Century« (15th and 16th centuries), in the »Século de Ouro«. She extended her influence – as the foremost European state – as far as India, China, and South America. Sometimes the medieval superpower even called the »Paço Real« in Sintra the middlepoint of the world. Associated with the much-visited Royal Palace are the names of Prince Henry the Navigator, Dom Manuel I (»Manuelism«), Luís de Camões – and the child-king Sebastião. When the word »Sebastianismo« is mentioned – in reference to this religious fanatic and source of many legends, who led his army on a hopeless campaign against the Arabs in North Africa, and who, since then (1578), is regarded as »missing« – it should be regarded as hinting at the inscrutability of the fatalistic Portuguese soul – pain, longing, and the merging of memory with hope for better times. These waves of feeling overflow in another form in the »Fado de Lisboa«. –

After the »Aviz« came the third and last monarchic dynasty, the house »Bragança«. Even before the founding of the Portuguese state, the Arabs had left their traces in Sintra, as Spanish rule also did intermittently, as well as Napoleon's troops and the Salazar regime in the 20th century. Timeless and exalted over all forms of rule are the words of the English poet Lord Byron, who saw a »Glorious Eden« in Sintra and its wonderful landscape, and who, in *Childe Harold's Pilgrimage,* composed his praise in verse:

»... Lo! Cintra's glorious Eden intervenes (...)
The horrid crags, by toppling convent crown'd,
The cork-trees hoar that clothe the shaggy steep,
The mountain-moss by scorching skies imbrown'd,
The sunken glen, whose sunless shrubs must weep,
The tender azure of the unruffled deep,
The orange tints that gild the greenest bough,
The torrents that from cliff to valley leap,
The vine on high, the willow branch below,
Mix'd in one mighty scene, with varied beauty glow ...«

The »Castelo dos Mouros«, a former Moorish fortress complex, is spread over rugged mountain ridges. And the »Palácio da Pena« is enthroned on a mountain peak, as well. This fairy-tale castle, for which the German architect Wilhelm Freiherr von Eschwege borrowed and combined the characteristics of all the styles known to him, was a present from Ferdinand von Sachsen-Coburg-Gotha (»Fernando«) to his Portuguese wife, Queen Maria Glória II. The »Palácio da Pena« is a public attraction.

The giant park surrounding it and the park »Monserrate« are impressive. Today, it is no longer obvious that the intricate gardens were artificially designed and laid out. In the meantime, over 2,000 species of plants from all over the world have grown together into a fantastic natural botanical garden. Were the ferns, now meters high, planted in the park »Monserrate« personally by James Cook, the English circumnavigator of the world? He, like so many of the British, is supposed to have found pleasure in the moist, mild, and often misty »Serra da Sintra«.

The broad »Quinta« properties sprawl behind enchanted high and ivy-covered walls. These are estates, named after their respective central, regal complexes of buildings, which latter are, however, seldom visible from the road. –

When the open air market in São Pedro de Sintra is held, an antique-lover's heart skips a beat.

The road from »Cabo da Roca« to Sintra passes through the white village Malveira da Serra. A steep climb through sparse forests with large, water-smoothed boulders and scree leads from there to the idyllic »Lagoa Azul«, one of the few lakes in the entire region.

Gardens at the »Palácio dos Seteais« at Sintra

The gentle peacefulness exuded by the »Serra da Sintra« is interrupted only when the international »Formula 1« auto races are held on the nearby »Autódromo do Estoril«.

From the downtown »Estação de Rossio« on their way to Sintra, the trains run through the Northwestern suburbs of Lisbon like »Amadora« and »Benfica«, which show clearly that their inhabitants have to work very hard for their livelihood. They also stop in »Queluz«, which means »What light!« This light illuminates the royal »Palácio Nacional de Queluz«, built in the 18th century, which gave its name to this suburb. After the earthquake of 1755, the final construction work on the originally definitely Baroque structure stretched out for years. Marquês de Pombal had not only diverted most builders and finances for the reconstruction of Lisbon, but the French architects' Rococo elements don't fit in the Rationalist concept that this Enlightenment man left as his lasting contribution to the face of »Queluz«. The »Portuguese Versailles« is embedded in broad gardens cultivated in the style of the French garden architects.

The »Mafra Convent«, which also dates from the 18th century, and which was built over a 13-year period, is in the town of the same name. King João V had sworn to have a magnificent building erected if his wife, the Austrian Maria Anna, gave birth to an heir to the throne. After the birth of the later Dom José I, the contract for the »Convento e Palácio de Mafra« was given to two German builders. With the help of 50,000 workers, Johann Friedrich Ludwig and his son Peter went to work building a complex containing a basilica, a cloister, and a palace, into whose 220 meter long front side the facade of a church is integrated, and which terminates in a cupola that looks »Early Bavarian«. (The builders came from Southern Germany.) 882 halls and rooms are distributed through the complex, and 114 bells can all be rung at the same time. The library comprises some 30,000 volumes, and serves more as decoration than to quench anyone's thirst for knowledge.

Few monks lived here; today part of the tract has been remodelled into a barracks. The royal family never felt at home in Mafra.

The heir to the throne, Dom José I, has gone down in history as the »Reformer«. During his reign, the earthquake of 1755 destroyed Lisbon and many other parts of the country. His minister Marquês de Pombal restructured and reformed Portugal and Lisbon in many fields, and the king's title »Reformador« was actually earned by his energetic minister. When the king died, the Marquês quickly fell from favor.

The Mafra-architect Johann Friedrich Ludwig became a naturalized Portuguese under the name Ludowice. His building was financed with Brazilian gold. But there never has been enough money for the adequate upkeep of the complex.

Dom João V wasn't simply interested in keeping his oath. The Mafra Convent was also built in rivalry with the monastic palace »El Escorial«, near Madrid. Everything in Mafra was to be more beautiful, more impressive, and more splendid than in »El Escorial«. In any case, Mafra's palatial cloister was built bigger.

*Located high in the »Serra de Sintra«, the »Palácio da Pena«
exhibits widely differing styles of castle and palace
architecture*

*The long ascent to the »Palácio da Pena« leads through a romantic,
thickly-grown park landscape with a great variety of species
up to a terrace with a wide view of the vegetation veiled in fog*

121

*The »Serra de Sintra«, with its thick vegetation
and, in the heights, heavy cloud banks,
keeps storm clouds away from Lisbon*

*The »Mafra« Convent impresses with its huge
dimensions and commands respect
with its massive architecture*

Ericeira and the Praias

Lisbon's Beautiful Beaches

A characteristic fishing boat has been towed into the street

A birds'-eye-view reveals how the white-golden beaches blend into the blue expanse of the Atlantic Ocean. This image is often obscured from the land side by the steep cliffs on the coast.

The harbor and the wide curves of the breakwater in the booming beach town Ericeira are just as picturesque from the air as on the ground. Nets, anchors, and the typical colorful ships create a maritime ambience followed up by the famous »Marisco« restaurants of the town. At its core, it is still a fishing village. The cutters, barges, skiffs, and other boats are towed and docked far up the steep alleys, almost in the middle of town. In Ericeira, the last Portuguese king, Manuel II, left the country with his family on his yacht when, on October 5, 1910, a putsch supplanted the monarchy with the first Portuguese republic. The king steered toward Gibraltar from Ericeira and went from there into British exile.

The waves of the Atlantic crash on Ericeira's beaches, which lie below long stretches of steep bluffs. The breezes, often quite strong, provide refreshing coolness even on hot summer days.

The course of the coast South of Ericeira along the »Cabo da Roca« to the »Guincho« introduces one to the »Praia da Adraga« in the vicinity of Almoçagene and its bizarre rock formations. – The »Praia Grande« and the »Praia Pequena« each have their own charm; likewise the »Praia das Maçãs« – the »Apples Beach«. The prosperous beach town of the same name unfolds its charms even in winter. Then, however, the rails are no longer ridden by the pretty, almost open-sided Oldtimer streetcar, whose depot is in Branzão. The classically beautiful streetcar used to go directly from Sintra to »Praia das Maçãs«.

The apple barges once docked in Colares on the Rio das Maçãs to unload their ware.

This seaside town still lends its name to a particular wine. »Colares« is one of the ten defined wine regions of Portugal; a ruby red wine is grown here. Its vines grow quite low and have to be protected from being burnt by the hot sand. The name of Carcavelos, a town with a broad beach on the Lisbon coast, also doubles as the name of a »Região Demarcada«. This small winegrowing region produces heavy Southern wines, similar to those grown in the region of Setúbal. The latter harbor and industrial city lies on the Rio Sado in the South of the »Serra da Arrábida« – in the very broadest sense »na outra banda«, on the »other side« of the Rio Tejo.

»Na outra banda«

The Costa da Caparica

During the winter, the broad beaches on the
»Costa da Caparica« belong to the sea birds.
In the long summer period, the »Lisboetas«
ensure continuous action

The Christ statue »Cristo Rei« is already »na outra banda« – on the other shore of the Rio Tejo. The ferries from »Terreiro do Paço« and from the docking stations in »Belém« come here after Cacilhas and Trafaria. But the main traffic artery is the bridge – »a Ponte«. Its Southern end »na outra banda« is already located on the Arrábida Peninsula. The »Península« extends, on the sea side, for about 30 kilometers along the gently falling, sandy »Costa da Caparica« and thus reveals another kind of landscape than the steep, rocky coast between Cascais and Ericeira in the Northwest of the capital.

The coastline runs as far as the »Lagoa de Albufeira«. This lake is a paradise for water sports and lies deeply embedded in the mountainous topography of the »Península da Arrábida«, between forests, dunes, and a small village. Soon the coast jumps around lonely »Cabo Espichel« and continues from an impressively beautiful and lofty rock formation to the mouth of the Rio Sado. –

During the hot summer months, the »Costa da Caparica« is a heavily-populated goal for outings for big-city people of all ages. The long jetties divide the coast into many small beaches.

A large bus station with shade-giving awnings is near the end station of the little beach train. The latter takes wide loops to cover the swimming coves, which stretch for kilometers.

In the winter, when only a few people stroll past the closed-up little summer houses like visitors to an abandoned gold rush town, and when the empty beaches belong only to the gulls and a few hardy windsurfers, the »Costa da Caparica« develops a very special charm. The healthy sea air and the Atlantic, whose waves usually seem, from a distance, to roll up quite gently, are a picture of peaceful contemplation standing in stark contrast to the turbulence of the tourist season.

Steep Shores

*Between the Cabo
Espichel and the
Serra da Arrábida*

The Arrábida Peninsula, with its widely varied landscapes, is one of the »Lisboetas'« favorite goals for outings. On its Southern coast, in Sesimbra, they meet up with the foreign tourists. The former fishing village has developed into a city full of vacation apartments extending from the beach up to the slopes of the mountain. But the »Lota«, the fish auction, proves that the fishermen are still an essential aspect of Sesimbra. The picturesque spot is crowned with the ruins of an old Moorish castle, which offers a view far across the land and ocean. –

On the impressive plateau of the »Cabo Espichel«, a long road ends on the huge grounds of a former cloister and church for pilgrims. Once a year, in October, people celebrating the fishermen's festival crowd the area. Solitude reigns the rest of the time, in harmony with the dignified, barren, wave-beaten cliffs. Far below, the Atlantic has been breaking off rock since long before memory. A squat little white chapel fits in beautifully with the fissured stone columns that seem like prehistoric monuments – but they were recently erected by Portuguese artists.

The immense lighthouse on a further extension of the »Cabo Espichel« seems like a twin of the beacon at the »Cabo da Roca«, far away in the Northwest of the capital, whose silhouette one can almost make out at the horizon's intersection of ocean and sky. When the sun gradually sinks in the sea, and the lighthouses all along the Lisboan Coast begin to blink in the long, red-orange dusk, and more and more fishing boats out on the waters light their lanterns, the beauty of it all is more than any visitor could ever forget. –

In the South of the peninsula, the ridges of the »Serra da Arrábida« ball up to another rapidly rising coast that falls steeply into the ocean. Going through the nature preserve of the »Mata do Solitário« and its lushly varied vegetation, one arrives at the deep bay of Portinho da Arrábida. The shore roads and ridge roads are some of the most beautiful coastal routes in the country. They also lead past a white »Convento«. The cloister is gently embedded in a slope and surrounded with wilderness and forest for kilometers in all directions.

From the high mountain ridges, one looks simultaneously over the dark blue, broad ocean and into the valley landscapes of the »Península da Arrábida«, and, on clear days, even the »White City« Lisbon can be made out in the distance.

The »Serra da Arrábida« falls in a long curve. Setúbal, the third largest city and port in Portugal (after Lisbon and Porto), spreads out in the foothills on the Rio Sado. The work in the shipyards and sardine canneries dominates the rhythm and appearance of the city, but the many colorful cottages and freshly painted wooden boats in the harbor, seen at the city's entrance, are part of the scene as well. Here, Setúbal still conveys the impression of a fishing village. The actual harbor area is unadorned; instead, it is characterized by sober business – as is the whole city.

The fine »Miradouro« above the entrance to the harbor obscures how important the export companies that have offices here and everywhere on the Portuguese coast are for Setúbal. This port city wrestles constantly for its share of the export of wood and cork, of textiles, foodstuffs or half-finished products. Setúbal has never been rich, and the necessary industries have carved deeper wrinkles in Setúbal's face than elsewhere. Setúbal, hit even harder than Lisbon by the earthquake of 1755, nonetheless long ago developed a contemporary inner city. Some streets have been reserved for pedestrians only, and many of these meet at the »Praça du Bocage«, named for the popular poet. The church São Julião survived the earthquake, as did the Jesus Church, whose Manuelistic portal outside and whose »Azulejo« pictures inside attract deserved attention. The port city has a copious Oceanographic Museum with one of the world's largest collection of sponges. –

Auto ferries dock in Setúbal and sail to the kilometer-long, slender spit of land that divides the bay at the mouth of the Rio Sado and the fresh water in the Northeast from the seawater in the West.

With its Greek name of Tróia, the former Roman »Cetóbriga« has given its name to the entire geologically unique tongue of land. Only a few ruins remain from the Roman settlement, which was destroyed in 412 by a flood.

Contemporary Tróia is well-known as one of the largest and most modern of Portugal's vacation resorts. The large vacation homes, the diverse vacation facilities, and the beautiful golf course directly beside the sea all have good reputations among the Portuguese, who come with their families from all over the country here to the »Península de Tróia« and to its long white beaches lined with pine forests. The ferry lines to and from Setúbal are an important part of the transportation artery connecting Tróia directly with Lisbon.

Even with a backdrop of empty vacation homes and cottages, the town and the »Costa Caparica« unfold a melancholy charm in winter

The beacon fire in the mouth of the Rio Tejo
indicates the two shipping channels
formed by sand banks

*The beach town »Costa da Caparica«
takes its name from the kilometer-long coast
so well-visited in the summer*

*Behind the chapel on the lonely, wind-scoured
plateau of the »Cabo Espichel«,
the cliffs fall deep down into the Atlantic*

Returning –
The other Entrée in the Capital

From Palmela to the Cacilheiros

At Palmela, the highway from Setúbal to Lisbon intersects the connection from »Cabo Espichel« to Montijo – that industrial city on the other side of the huge Rio Tejo basin that is sailed to from the ferry station on the »Praça do Comércio«, the »Cais da Alfândega«.

On its Northern side, the »Serra da Arrábida« falls toward the plains. Only the idyllic village Palmela is perched 250 meters high like an eagle's aerie on one of the last mountain peaks. From the central »Castelo«, one looks out over the whitewashed town and past its intricate alleys westward over the flatlands. The castle was the mightiest Moorish fortress in Southern Portugal and was intended to guard the approaches to Lisbon.

After the Christians had regained Portugal from the Moors in the course of the »Reconquista«, the »Castelo« of Palmela was converted into a knights' castle and cloister. Even today, one can still get goosebumps peering into the deep »Dry Cistern«, in which Dom João II imprisoned the Bishop of Évora and his numerous followers until they were executed. The representatives of the Church and nobility had revolted against the king's new plans of reform (1484). The comfortable luxury of the »Pousada Castelo de Palmela« – surely one of the most exquisite and beautiful hotels of its kind – has long since moved into the formerly Spartan cloister cells. –

The roads lead back to Cacilhas again – the starting point for outings on the »Península da Arrábida«. Lisbon announces itself from afar. More and more housing developments emerge near Almada and Cacilhas, extending these suburbs outward to the South, sometimes completely obliterating the cores of old towns.

The population density increases, and soon the back of the »Cristo Rei« statue is in sight. In Cacilhas, one is almost in Lisbon again. The capital awaits its inhabitants, its visitors – whether after crossing the »Ponte« or after a ferry ride, with its sea smells, on a »Barco Cacilheiro« to the »Estação Fluvial« on the »Cais do Sodré«.

To look out now from a »Miradouro« in Lisbon at the silhouette of the heights of the »Serra da Arrábida«, seemingly so far removed, is to know that the capital has projected its alter ego »na outra banda« – »to the other side«. There are wrinkles on this second face of Lisbon, but even more laugh lines – as with the capital itself: a metropolis that lives without cosmetics.

Whoever chose to journey from the mountainous Atlantic port through the »Península da Arrábida« can look forward to a great entrée upon his return. The honorable »White City« opens up with outstretched, greeting arms at the Rio Tejo:

»Bem-Vindo a Lisboa!«

»Welcome to Lisbon!«

Photo credits

Manfred Hamm
Cover (Dust Jacket), Page 2/3, 4/5, 6/7, 8/9, 10, 20, 25, 30, 31, 34 (right), 35, 36, 37, 40, 41, 42, 43, 44, 57, 58, 59, 60, 61, 65, 66 (two photos), 69, 71, 72, 76, 77, 79, 80, 81, 87, 93, 98, 99, 100, 101, 102, 103, 106, 120, 121, 122/123, 124, 135

Werner Radasewsky
Page 17, 23, 24, 26, 27, 28, 29, 32, 33, 34 (left), 38, 39, 45, 47, 48, 49, 51, 52, 53, 55, 63, 64, 67 (two photos), 68, 70, 73, 74, 78, 82, 83, 85, 86, 88, 89, 91, 92, 96, 97, 105, 107, 108, 109, 110, 111, 113, 114, 115, 116, 117, 119, 125, 126, 127, 128, 129, 131, 132, 133, 134, 137, Back Cover (Dust Jacket)